SUSANNE EVERETT
LONDON
THE GLAMOUR YEARS 1919-39

SUSANNE EVERETT

LONDON
THE GLAMOUR YEARS 1919-39

GALLERY BOOKS
An imprint of W.H. Smith Publishers Inc.
112 Madison Avenue
New York, New York 10016

A Bison Book

Published by Gallery Books
A Division of W.H. Smith Publishers Inc.
112 Madison Avenue
New York, New York 10016

Produced by
Bison Books Corp.
17 Sherwood Place
Greenwich, CT 06830

ISBN 0-8317-9933-1

Printed in Hong Kong

1   2   3   4   5   6   7   8   9   10

Page 1: A group of young ladies and their escort enjoying
themselves at Ascot, June 1925.
Page 2-3: Oxford Circus bustling with life, 5 May 1928.
Below: Enjoying the races at Henley Regatta, July 1924.

Contents

The Old Order

Near the end of Part II of Galsworthy's *A Modern Comedy*, an elderly Marquis surveys his errant, debt-ridden granddaughter. 'I should have liked', he said, 'to ask you not to cheapen our name any more, but I suppose that would be putting the clock back. The spirit of the age is against me.' His granddaughter stared at him uncomprehendingly. 'The spirit of the age! It was all very well, but he didn't understand what it was. Cheapen? Why! She had raised the price of the family name: hoicked it out of a dusty cupboard and made of it a current coin. People sat up when they read of her. Did they sit up when they read of grandfather? But he would never see that. . . .'

It would have been surprising if he could, for the Honourable Marjorie Ferrars and her noble grandfather were separated by more than the tensions induced by the censoriousness of the old towards the young. They were divided by a far more unbridgeable chasm, into whose depths had been sucked the residue of British imperialist dreams, and from the horror of which those who took part were never fully to recover – the First World War.

The eighty-year-old Marquis of Shropshire, his aristocratic feet firmly planted in the

soil of Victorian England, was unlikely to be much in sympathy with his rootless, painted, shingled, chain-smoking granddaughter. As he pointed out, to settle her debts he would have to sell the Gainsborough, for 'times are hard, land costs money, collieries cost money, Shropshire House costs money; and where's the money?' Could he, he wondered, rely on her 'word as a lady' that she would pay ready money in the future? Marjorie, a realist to the last, reassured him. 'Alright, dear, I'll be careful. I think I'll go to America.' Her grandfather was still not convinced. 'And start a fashion of marrying American husbands? It's not yet been done, I believe. . . . Just one thing, Marjorie. I'm eighty, and you're – what are you – twenty five? Don't get through life so fast – you'll be dreadfully bored by the time you're fifty, and there's no greater bore than a bored person. . . .'

This last accusation was not, however, entirely fair. Keeping boredom at bay had always been a problem for the very rich, and the pursuit of pleasure had always been an extremely serious business. The Duke of Portland, on succeeding to the title in 1879, was interviewed by his commanding officer, who advised him to be 'a bit of a jack-of-all-trades. Don't just stick to hunting and sport, but try and enjoy everything as it comes. Always intersperse your pleasure with business, and then things that might otherwise bore you will act as spice to your enjoyment.' Edward VII, too, despite the obvious enjoyment he

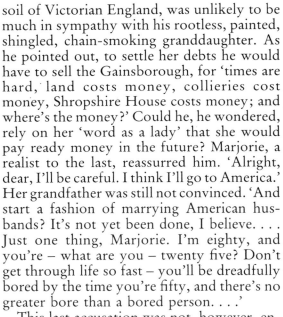

got from being a king after so many years of adapting himself to the stringent demands of his mother, Queen Victoria, was alarmingly prone to boredom. Terrified hostesses, seeing the all-too-familiar danger signals, 'eyelids falling, voice deepening and slowing up, fingers drumming on the arm of his chair', would rush some vivacious beauty to his side to entertain him.

The dreadful threat of *ennui* had to be averted. For the children of the old century, born into a world in which the fixed order of things seemed as immutable as death, the vacuum created by the loss, not only of many

Balfour. "HERE, I SAY! HELP! WHAT ON EARTH IS IT? ANOTHER OF THESE AWFUL LABOUR MEMBERS?"
C.-B. "NOT EXACTLY, MY DEAR ARTHUR; THIS IS JUST A *CLEAN SWEEP*"

Above: A Liberal candidate appeals to a group of workers in the 1906 Campaign.

own house, filled with Chinese statues, Maillots and Goyas, with a Boucher in the bathroom. Rather would they echo the world-weary sentiments of another character in *Antic Hay*, Mrs Viveash, who complained that since the war all things, even formerly delectable treats such as lobster, or wine, or 'those soft caramels they call Fiats' had lost their savour. 'Nothing's the same now,' she added, sadly, 'and I feel it never will be.'

The changes were, indeed, profound, but they were as much to do with disillusionment as with shifts in nationality, political status or altered economic expectations. For when the Western powers finally laid down their arms in 1918 it was in impoverishment and bloodshed; the 'war to end wars', begun in a welter of stirring speeches for reasons of alliance, patriotism and dreams of liberation, had ended in ugliness and despair. The England to which the battered survivors returned was not the one they had left and it was one in which uncertainty and cynicism replaced confidence and trust. Nobody who had fought and lived on the battlefields of Ypres or the Somme would ever again believe in man's ultimate humanity to man, and for them and for the mourning relatives of the one million dead the 'land fit for heroes' was a poor substitute for the world they had lost.

Nostalgia for the quiet haven of the late Victorian and Edwardian eras has never left the British. The longing to recapture past imperial grandeurs and to relive the order and stability of the thirty years before 1914 are as strong now as they have ever been. It was, perhaps, to re-create the atmosphere of pre-First World War Europe that England joined the European Community that single, civilised community of which A J P Taylor wrote so eloquently, in which a man could:

'travel across the length and breadth of the Continent without a passport until he reached the frontiers of Russia and the Ottoman Empire . . . [where he could] settle in a foreign country for work or leisure without legal formalities . . . [where] every currency was as good as gold, though this security rested ultimately on the skill of financiers in the City of London . . . [where] private property was everywhere secure. . . .

He might have added that the British, in particular, did not only have Europe as their playground. Beyond its borders they could look north, south, east and west towards infinitely large and rich tracts of land inhabited by subject peoples over whom they held absolute sway. From Canada to the Caribbean, from the Mediterranean to the Cape, from India to New Zealand they could wander as they pleased, their suzerainty unquestioned, their *droits de seigneurs* god-like in their omnipotency.

of the assets that had bolstered up the elaborate structure of their lives, but also of fathers, brothers, and friends killed during the war, could be filled only by even more frenzied attempts to allay the tedium of occupying the endless waking hours.

'What are you up to Fanny?', asked Polly in Nancy Mitford's *Love in a Cold Climate*. 'Aching' was the reply, meaning aching with boredom, a malaise from which girls, before national service came to their rescue, were apt to suffer considerably. Not for them the innocent fantasies of Aldous Huxley's schoolmaster, Mr Gumbril, who only asked to meet his mistress in the Ritz, or to move about his

Right: A poster used by the Liberals in 1906 appeals to the electorate's democratic sentiments.

Far right top: A fox hunt at the Earl of Fitzwilliam's country seat in Clumber.

Far right bottom: The bag after a good day's shoot at Studley Royal, 1911. The offer of good shooting enticed many visitors to accept invitations to spend Saturday to Monday in the country.

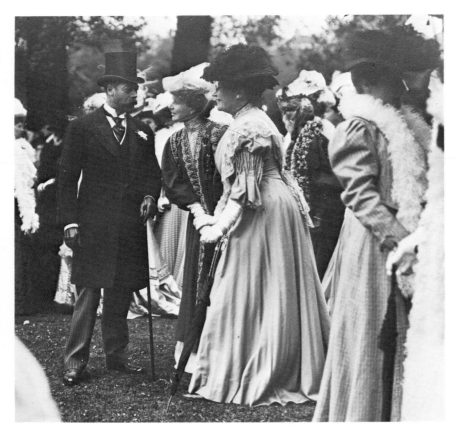

and dreams of colour and excitement, were the English upper-middle classes. The intoxicating prospect of exercising Olympian powers over lesser breeds without the law, coupled with romantic yearnings induced by visions of viceregal palaces, jewelled elephants and limitless servants, inspired many a young man fresh from Harrow, Rugby or Haileybury to take up the white man's burden. It was not only the promise of material comforts that beckoned them. There was also an overriding sense of purpose for, by offering their services to their Queen Empress they would become, as one headmaster put it in the 1890s, 'citizens of the greatest Empire under heaven and as such must have faith in the divinely ordered mission of their country and their race.'

This sense of imperial mission had not always been so fervently endorsed. Before the Indian Mutiny in 1858 – an uprising which convinced the British that without their leavening presence the empire would revert to barbarism – a certain amount of snobbishness was shown towards those who chose to seek their fortunes in the Colonies. Gentlemen, it was felt, did not need to make money.

Above: The Prince of Wales chats to a guest at a Royal garden party at Marlborough House in 1907.

Undaunted by difficulties of terrain, climate or language, and unshaken in their conviction that they had a mission to convert the heathen, the British straddled their empire with a confidence and panache unseen since the Romans. This vast colossus remained intact until the end of the First World War, after which, despite the euphoria of victory and the acquisition of many former German colonies, the heart went out of the British Empire. The flames of imperialism could not be rekindled and old men assessing the possibilities of imperial federation (one answer to the prevailing orthodoxy of President Wilson's concept of self-determination, or the 'right of every people to decide its own future') were howled down by their juniors, 'Not the beastly old Empire *again*. . . . My sainted aunt, you'd think we were still fighting the fuzzy-wuzzies. . . .'

Until then, however, the edifice had few cracks. The Boer War had been a bit of a setback: a few people began to ask themselves whether they had the right to subjugate the weak in the interests of the strong, and one or two wondered if the ruling classes had behaved as impeccably as they should (tales of the Guards seen 'running for their lives through the South African night' provided an unwelcome reminder that the aphorism 'one Englishman can beat two foreigners' might not be altogether true), but on the whole the structure was sound.

The prop and mainstay of this edifice, the practical rulers who set sail with high ideals

'They all say Nabobs are enormously rich', whispered Rebecca in *Vanity Fair*. Rich he may have been, but the fat, self-indulgent ex-collector of Boggley Wallah was not spared by Thackeray, who lampooned him with merciless glee. His fondness for chillies, his talk of *punkahs* and *tatties*, his provinciality, all showed him up as a figure of fun, a gigantic anachronism, ill at ease in refined society.

After 1858 these class scruples disappeared in a wave of patriotic ardour. 'You were not', as Jonathan Gathorn Hardy said, 'going out to get rich, but for the good of your country.' Nevertheless, despite these changes in social attitude, recruits to the Indian Civil Service and Colonial Service were drawn mainly from the educated middle class. The landed gentry, with a few notable exceptions (Lord Canning, Lord Curzon and Lord Cromer), were reluctant to abandon their estates for the uncertainties of far-flung lands, however highly regarded such a course of action might be. An Indian maharajah, visiting Kedleston Hall in Derbyshire, seat of the Curzon family, expressed just such an opinion. Lost in admiration for its magnificence, he

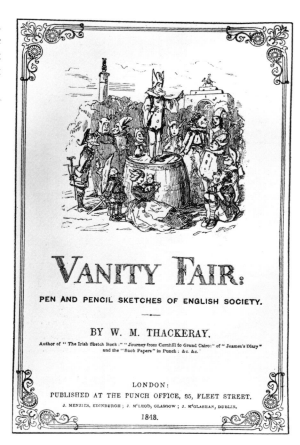

Left: The cover of Thackeray's *Vanity Fair*. Thackeray lampooned English society in his writings, attacking class prejudices and the provincialism of the aspiring middle classes.

Below: Developing industries made vast profits for landowners far-sighted enough to invest in them. The profits from Coalbrookdale, pictured here, allowed Sir John Guest to renovate and modernize his house at Canford.

wondered that Englishmen ever 'went to India at all, when they could stay at home in such a place, playing the flute and watching the rabbits.'

In any case, the fact remained that they were a great deal more comfortable at home, for home was both an expression of taste and a platform for political ambition. Although the power enjoyed by the aristocracy had greatly diminished by the middle of the nineteenth century, many landowners, by investing in by-products of the Industrial Revolution, managed to comfort themselves with the thought that even if their grip on the country's institutions was slowly slipping from their grasp into the hands of upstart bankers and cotton manufacturers, at least they were none the poorer for it.

Some became a great deal the richer. In 1870 the first Duke of Westminster spent £600,000 remodelling his 'ignorant and frivolous Gothic' mansion, Eaton Hall, after discovering a copper mine on his estate. The second Duke, the formidable and capricious Bendor, had, by the time he died in 1935, enriched the Grosvenor family by some £16 million through a judicious series of invest-

ments. In the 1890s the Duke of Portland invested in a 'wide range of industrial debentures and ordinary shares, taking in home breweries, collieries and stores, South African Gold mines and Burmese, Indian and South American railways; by 1907 the nominal value of his personal holdings was over £75,000.' The iron industries of Wales and Coalbrookdale supplied the money for the facelift given to Canford by Sir John Guest.

It was all very well, however, for peers to appear on the boards of railway companies, breweries or mines, or to dabble in rubber and gold, but the first thing a self-made man felt it necessary to do was to put at least a hundred miles between the source of his wealth and his domain. There, ensconced in his custom-built Wagnerian pile, resplendent with turrets and gables and surrounded by a respectable amount of land, he prepared to lead the life of a country gentleman.

This, as he soon found, was by no means an easy matter. Prejudices abounded. However hard he tried, however many churches, alms-houses, parish halls, schools or model cottages he built, however circumspectly he dressed, however much he rode, shot or fished, however much money he diverted into the right political channels, he always came up against one insurmountable obstacle - he had acquired his money by ungentlemanly means.

The old eighteenth-century adages that 'a gentleman is a man who has no occupation' and that his attitude to money should be one of 'lordly indifference' still clung, as did the view that no-one who had not been born and bred to the high estate of a landed aristocrat could lay claim to his virtues. Honour, dignity, integrity, courtesy, consideration and chivalry were held to be qualities difficult to acquire unless centuries of subordination to the traditional values of country and public life had ironed out all traces of roughness.

'My own personal misfortune', wrote Kenneth Clark in his autobiography, 'was an exceptionally stupid housemaster . . . who took a great dislike to me because I was not a gentleman, and ecouraged his prefects to beat me more, even, than they felt inclined to do.' Kenneth Clark's father inherited a thriving thread business, so thriving that when he married in 1901 he owned a London house in Grosvenor Square, a twenty-five bedroomed country house in Suffolk, surrounded by a park which even 'making allowance for the magnifying glass of memory must have been fairly large' and 'several' yachts. He rented a house in Scotland and later built a villa at Mentone. His shooting parties were conducted on lines that rivalled the Duke of Westminster's shoots in Wales where 'ten thousand pheasants were driven across from

Below: Sir Ernest Cassel in the robes of the Order of St Michael and St George. An industrialist who made a great fortune, he owed his acceptance into London Society to the countenance of King Edward VII, who did much to break down traditional barriers against self-made men.

one valley to another' and the guns were fed by an army of servants who brought out hayboxes filled with local oysters and liver pâté, steak-and-kidney pudding, cold turkey and ham, treacle tart, double Cottenham cheese and plum cake, washed down with claret and kümmel. Everything he did and everything he owned was on a scale rivalled by only the richest of aristocrats. This, however, was not enough to turn either him or his son into a gentleman.

It mattered little to Mr Clark. He was fond of saying that 'nobody with a title ever wrote to him, except to ask for money,' it mattered even less to his son, who went up to Oxford and pursued his career as an aesthete unencumbered by any sense of social stigma.

Neither did questions of this kind much affect King Edward VII's financial and mercantile friends, Sir Ernest Cassel, Sir Thomas Lipton and Sir Blundell Maple, although they were all aware of the mixed feelings with which they were viewed by London society. As Philip Magnus said: 'Politics and Society were intertwined traditionally, but financiers and merchants owed much to the countenance of the Prince of Wales.' Sir Ernest Cas-

Left and below: Sir Thomas Lipton *(left)* increased his fortune by opening a chain of grocery stores. The first one, opened in Glasgow in the 1890s, is seen below. He was a great friend of Edward VII and, despite his mercantile background, was knighted in 1898.

sel, in particular, took, as one historian put it, 'an aloof and realistic attitude to the society which fawned upon him. Social life to him was a means and not an end. . . .' Nevertheless he both enjoyed and courted honours – one of his conditions for loaning half a million pounds to the State Bank of Morocco was that he should receive the Grand Cross of the Order of the Bath, a request rather grudgingly complied with by the King, who was said to be 'displeased'.

Even the Rothschilds, whose enormous wealth, combined with a chameleon-like capacity to absorb themselves into the fabric of English life had almost removed any taint of foreignness or vulgarity from their name, occasionally found themselves glad of royal patronage. In 1889 Lord (Nathanial) Rothschild was offered the appointment of Lord Lieutenant of Buckinghamshire, in succession to the last Duke of Buckingham, a move strongly resisted by Lord Carrington. The Prince of Wales, on whose recommendation Lord Rothschild was appointed, wrote his friend a placatory letter, 'It would have been strange ten years ago, but times change. He is a good fellow and a man of business, and he and his family own half the country.'

However, if the bastions of privilege had been breached to some extent by this fresh blood circulating in society, the backbone remained the same. For all the entrepreneurial finess of the new men, it was the old order that made the rules. The new boys could only try and play the game as well as they were able.

Sir Julius Wernher, with his fortune from South African diamonds, was eager to adopt the outward conventions of the old aristocracy. He bought Luton Hoo, Beatrice Webb wrote, because 'part of the minor convention of his life has been the acquisition of a great country mansion,' with an historic name as counterpart of Bath House, Piccadilly.' Having bought it, he sought the company of those from whom he had drawn his inspiration: members of aristocratic and socially brilliant groups like the Souls, among whom were Lord Balfour, Lord Curzon, Lord Lyttleton, Lady Frances Horner, Lady Mary Jeune, Margot Tennant and her sister Lady Ribblesdale. While outwardly deploring the air of rich vulgarity and oppulence, 'There might just well have been a Goddess of Gold erected for overt worship', recorded Beatrice Webb disapprovingly, after dining at Bath House with Sir Julius Wernher and a 'company of financial magnates and their hangers-on', the aristocrats were bound to admit in secret that there was something unpleasantly alluring about the sight of all that glittering money.

The unmentionable subject of money cropped up distressingly often. Agricultural incomes had dropped alarmingly towards the end of the nineteenth century, due to the anti-corn lawn campaign and the agitation for free trade in land, and buried deep in the psyche of every aristocrat was a plutocrat struggling to get out. Egged on by sympathetic songs such as that sung at the annual tenants' dinner of the Percey family, which declared roundly that

That social yoke with one accord
That binds the Peasant to his Lord
And Liberty that idle vaunt
Is not the Comfort that we want

many a duke looked around for ways and means to supplement his income. One of these was the American wife.

Across the Atlantic, linked by ties of race and creed, was Fifth Avenue, New York. Lining each side of this prestigious avenue were mansions of a size to dwarf even the most elaborate in Grosvenor Square. They belonged to the Vanderbilts, the Smith Butlers, the Vincent Astors, the Barklie McKees, the Clay Fricks and the Sheldon Whitehouses. All were rich and all belonged to the 'best set' in America. Theirs, as Cornelius Vanderbilt observed, was the 'aged-in-the wood money, made in railroads, banking, tobacco and cotton, years before the Battle of Gettysburg.'

For them, money was a discreet but necessary evil. They refused to disclose the network of their business connections, hidden under the aliases of holding companies and investment trusts. As Mrs Vanderbilt said, 'It takes at least three generations to wash off oil and two to exterminate the smell of hogs. . . .' They belonged to the Backbone of American

Society, that is to say, the seventy five stalwarts who were always invited to important functions. There was another list, consisting of a further one hundred and fifty names, entitled 'The Outer Fringe of American Society'. These unfortunates were only recognized because of their immense wealth or political power or standing in the community and were relegated to larger affairs, such as balls or charity bazaars, and were never invited to dinner.

All of these appeared very desirable to impoverished English aristocrats. There was only one snag. Were these heiresses, many of whom were undeniably ravishing to look at, really fit to join their exalted ranks? Would they quieten down and become truly English in manner and deportment? Were they as yet too brash in their ideas of social intercourse? In their turn the mothers of these rich prizes guarded their daughters with jealous pride and hunted their prey with the calculating cunning of lionesses. Any aristocrat would not do. Younger sons, unless exceptionally well-endowed, were out of the question. Ordinary baronets had no hope. Earls were possible, marquises tempting and dukes a catch. They could afford to be choosy.

Left: Lady Randolph Churchill née Jennie Jerome, the beautiful American heiress.

Right: Lilian Hammersley married the 8th Duke of Marlborough; her dollars were put to good use when central heating was installed in Blenheim Palace.

Below: Mrs Keppel, the beautiful and charming companion of King Edward VII. Under Edward's reign the court became less stuffy. Women were allowed greater licence, especially if they were respectably married.

There was one serious snag that aspiring fortune hunters only discovered when it was too late. This was the extreme difficulty of getting money out of their parents-in-law. 'Marry a Fifth Avenue heiress', exclaimed one French marquis, 'Not on your life! The first thing I know her parents would expect me to work. And then when I tell them to go and jump in the lake, she will divorce me and call herself a Marchioness for the rest of her days.' Cornelius Vanderbilt was of much the same opinion:

When people talk to me in tones of civic indignation of this or that titled foreigner about to steal still another American fortune, my heart bleeds for the poor bridegroom. Let him try to corner even a single twenty-five cent piece belonging to that fortune! If I were a fortune hunter, I would go after the daughters of bootleggers and laundry racketeers but I would steer clear of Fifth Avenue, of those great families with telephone-exchange names, for fear they would squeeze out of me what little I possess. The social registers of New York, Philadelphia and Chicago are littered with American-born Princesses, Countesses and Marchionesses whose former husbands went back to Europe in tourist-third. The newspapers don't print their stores.

Aristocrats clever enough to avoid these pitfalls included Lord Randolph Churchill, who married Jennie Jerome, the daughter of Leonard Jerome, who had made a fortune on the Stock Exchange, and his brother, the - eighth Duke of Marlborough, who married an 'enormously rich and amiable' wife, Lilian Hammersley, whose dollars were put to good use installing central heating and electric light in Blenheim Palace. His successor married two Americans, one after the other, first Miss Consuelo Vanderbilt and second Gladys Deacon of Boston. The eighth Duke of Manchester also married a Vanderbilt, another Consuelo (godmother of the Duchess), and the handsome eighth Duke of Roxburghe carried off May Goelet and her millions to his castle near Kelso.

Far from appearing brash, these ladies achieved considerable success in society, which, with Edward VII at its head, laid great emphasis on beautiful young married women. The King's affair with the discreet and gifted Mrs Keppel allowed married women a licence, if a tacit one, to do much as they pleased, in sharp contrast to society life under Queen Victoria, where any sign of independent thought was frowned on.

Doing much as you pleased was both possible and profitable between 1901 and 1914. Indeed, it would have been considered unwise and foolish to do otherwise. When there was money to be made, tastes to be indulged and freedom to enjoy, why do anything else? Released from the tiresome Victorian conventions of philanthropy and soul saving and surrounded by the comforts that only a thriving empire could give, the upper classes settled down to the serious business of amusing themselves. Of course there were occasional rumblings that all was not well between England and Germany, and now and again there were uncomfortable reminders from the newly formed Labour party that the lower classes might not be entirely satisfied with their lot, but these pinpricks were not expected to change the status quo. 'Let the Socialists rail as they will' wrote the magazine *Queen*, 'but centuries of power and wealth have given us the chance to perfect our social system . . . our upper classes are the finest body of thinkers and livers in the world.'

A talent for living, and, indeed, a strong liver, were essential. Without them no member of society would have survived a week. If it was not Saturday to Monday in the country, it was dinners, parties, the opera and the theatre in London, or visits to damp Scottish castles weighed down by trunkloads of clothes, and all fuelled by gargantuan quantities of food and drink.

Not everyone ate as much as the King, whose appetite never flagged and who did full justice to every meal (even after breakfast, lunch and a lobster salad for tea he could manage a twelve-course dinner and he often ate some cold chicken just before going to bed) but to refuse to take advantage of such lavish hospitality would have seemed churlish. 'I suppose', wrote Kenneth Clark, 'that a serious-minded sociologist could describe me as the worthless product of a decadent system . . . I was brought up in this world at its most questionable; and I enjoyed it.'

It was still a world in which the strongholds of power were firmly in the grasp of the upper classes. The Edwardian franchise was very far from being wholly democratic. Under a third of adults were registered voters and women could not vote. Even after the Liberal landslide of 1906 the House of Commons consisted almost entirely of old Etonians and landowners, with a sprinkling of active businessmen, nearly half of whom were involved in finance or insurance. One historian wrote:

Below: Lord Curzon, a pillar of English Society, became Viceroy of India when only 39.

Royal Opera Covent Garden

Proprietors . The Grand Opera Syndicate, Ltd.
General Manager . Mr. NEIL FORSYTH
Musical Director . Mr. PERCY PITT

[1 9 1 1]
THIS EVENING'S PERFORMANCE

Tuesday, November 7th, at 8.30

THE RUSSIAN BALLET

Organised by M. SERGE DE DIAGHILEW
Choreographic Director : M. MICHEL FOKINE
Artistic Director ; M. ALEXANDRE BENOIS

LE PAVILLON D'ARMIDE

Scenes and Dances by M. FOKINE
Mmes. ANNA PAVLOVA
(By Arrangement with the Palace Theatre)
PILTZ, NIJINSKA, SCHOLLAR, WASILEWSKA
MM. NIJINSKY
ADOLF BOLM, CECCHETTI, FROMAN

LES SYLPHIDES

Scenes and Dances by M. FOKINE
Mme. ANNA PAVLOVA. M. NIJINSKY
(By Arrangement with the Palace Theatre)

LE CARNAVAL

Scenes and Dances by M. FOKINE
Mme. ANNA PAVLOVA
(By Arrangement with the Palace Theatre)
Mmes. PILTZ, SCHOLLAR, NIJINSKA
MM. NIJINSKY
BOLM, CECCHETTI, SERGEEF, SEMENOV

Conductor . M. PIERRE MONTEUX

Above: A programme of the evening's entertainment at Covent Garden in 1911. The London Season included visits to the theatre and ballet, as well as the opera.

Society in England is a national institution, with a central meeting point in London during the season ... its members have an extraordinarily wide acquaintance with one another from one end of the land to the other. They are connected by marriage ... and they are brought constantly together by entertainments in the capital and visits at country houses. Such a constitution gives to society great solidity and great influence. ...

It was a system that seemed destined to last for ever. But for the vagaries of fate and the ambitions of the Kaiser, it would certainly have lasted a while longer, if not for ever. There were a few ripples: the King died; the Labour party gained a few seats in the 1910 election; respectable women could be seen chained to railings in an effort to draw attention to their lack of a vote; but there was nothing to prepare the upper classes for war. When it came, the news was greeted with amazement and disbelief. *Queen* had mentioned the murder of the Archduke Franz Ferdinand, but had ignored the political implications, merely dwelling on the beauty of the requiem service. After it finally sank in that England was indeed at war with Germany, but that it was only expected to last three months, Society heaved a sigh of relief and settled down to enjoy the war.

'The whole thing', as Katharine Tynan said, 'was a lark in which everyone played soldiers – saluting officers, watching parades and sneering at the "disloyal shirkers" who had not joined the glorious fight.' Such insouciance was bound to end in tears. By the early months of 1915 the horrible suspicion was beginning to dawn that what was to have

Right: An 18-pounder opens fire on the Somme, August 1918. At first high society saw the war simply as a minor inconvenience, but by 1918 most families had lost at least one relative in the trenches.

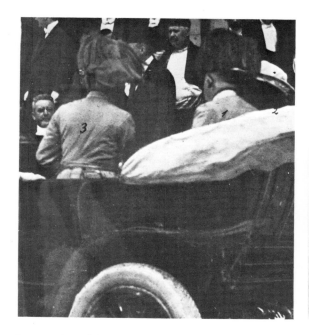

been a brief frolic was turning into a serious affair and it was one which showed no sign of ending. Dreary routine replaced light-hearted efforts at war work and austerity campaigns and rationing cast a gloomy shadow over London houses used to warmth and plenty. Afternoon bridge gave way to knitting parties and houses were turned into impromptu hospitals. Worse still, a steady roll call of deaths began to toll the passing of a generation.

The devastation wreaked by the First World War on the upper classes was without precedent. The shadow of death which hung over every family with a husband or a son at the front was rendered even more shocking by the comparative security of the past fifty years, when sudden death was so rare it was considered to be the greatest calamity of all. After 1914 it became a familiar spectre. Hardly a family was left untouched by tragedy and not even the fervent patriotism which led one feature writer to protest that 'those dead who had their chance to die thus are to be envied, *envied* from the bottom of our hearts, the hearts of us who sit at home in safety while they die for us . . .' could assuage their terrible grief. Some managed to put a brave face on it, if only in public. 'It became a point of honour', wrote Duff Cooper, 'never to show a sad face at the feast. And if we wept – as weep we did – we wept in secret.'

Gaiety in the teeth of disaster was seen as

Above, both: The Archduke Ferdinand with his wife at Sarajevo *(left)* just before their assassination which led to the outbreak of World War I, and *(above)* the murderer is captured.

Below: A ladies' Red Cross sewing meeting in 1914. The War helped change women's position in society and advanced the cause of universal suffrage.

the ultimate act of courage. As Duff Cooper wrote of Katharine Asquith, whose husband Raymond had been killed on the Somme in 1916: 'Her heart was broken but she did not wear black to prove it, and would have thought it wrong to cast the shadow of her comfortless sorrow over the fleeting moments of our gaiety.'

For a handful of lucky ones, the war was merely an inconvenient interruption to the social round. 'Drat the war', cried Sonia Keppel's nanny, 'It's upsetting everybody.' Sonia Keppel, the younger daughter of King Edward's favourite, came out in 1918, in the midst of her war work at a Forces' canteen. Although, as *Queen* pointed out glumly, 'the position of a town hostess in this time of war is not a very enviable one . . .' many were undeterred by the drastic economies in food, fuel and lighting. Candlelit dances and dinner parties were somehow managed by enterprising hostesses and *thé dansants* and afternoon visits to the cinema (albeit chaperoned by an acceptable married lady) provided suitable furtive delights for young girls. In the

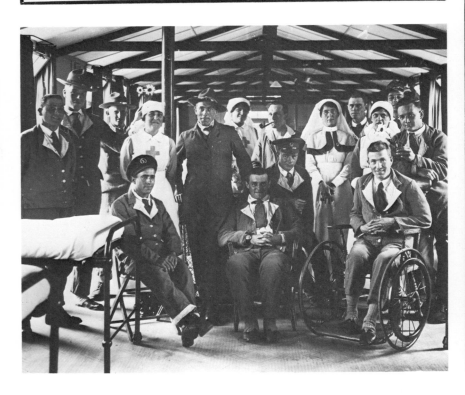

country, foxhunting was generally given up by 1917, but partridge and pheasant shoots continued on a reduced scale, as one observer recorded:

At Gorhambury, for instance, there was little gamekeeping staff left by 1918, so that practically no rabbits were shot in that season. But the bag of partridges and pheasants was kept up at little less than half its pre-war figure, and fairly frequent shooting parties were held throughout the war, with many officers among the guests.

Such shows of bravado caused more bitterness than respect. Bad feeling had already existed between those who stayed at home to work in munitions factories (or in any other capacity without displaying the qualifying badge signifying disablement or discharge) and those fighting at the front. After the war ended, the gulf widened even further. Demobilized men returning from abroad more often than not found their old jobs taken by someone else, 'usually a woman or a man who had escaped conscription', and no amount of palliatives in the form of free unemployment

Above: An illustration from *The Illustrated London News* in 1916 depicts troops enjoying their Christmas leave at Victoria Station.

Top far left: An advertisement from *The Illustrated London News* of 1916 highlights the problem of finding, and affording, servants in the war years, a problem which was to continue after the war.

Bottom far left: A group of wounded soldiers in London in 1918.

Left: Londoners celebrate Armistice Day, 11 November 1918.

24

reported in March 1919 that there had been a 'revolution in landowning' (one million acres were said to have been sold during that year). In 1920 the Duke of Rutland sold both 28,000 acres 'or about half' his Belvoir estate and the 12,500-acre estate of Scarisbrick in Lancashire. *The Times* wrote:

We all know it now, England is changing hands. . . . Will a profiteer buy it? Will it be turned into a school or an institution? Has the mansion house electric light and modern drainage? For the most part the sacrifices are made in silence. . . . The sons are perhaps lying in far-away graves; the daughters secretly mourning someone dearer than a brother, have taken up some definite work away from home, seeking thus to still their aching hearts, and the old people, knowing there is no son or near relative left to keep up the old traditions, or so crippled by necessary taxation that they know their boy will never be able to carry on when they are gone, take the irrevocable step.

It remained to be seen what was to survive. For the wild jubilation of the Armistice celebrations did more than express relief at the ending of a just war. They symbolized the end of an era, and no amount of self-pity on the part of the upper classes could bring it back. As Henry Asquith said in his address of congratulation to King George V: 'The old world has been laid waste. Principalities and Powers, to all appearances inviolable and invincible, which seem to dominate a large part of the families of mankind, lie in the dust. All things have become new.'

Above: Suffragettes chain themselves to the railings outside 10 Downing Street. They refused to be bound over to keep the peace and were therefore imprisoned for six months. However, after the war women were given the vote.

Right: Joyful Londoners celebrate the Armistice on board a London bus in 1918.

Facing page, both: Troops parade past the Cenotaph *(top)* and British tanks in procession in Westminster Bridge Road *(bottom)* in July 1919 as part of London's Peace Pageant. Few then realized the long-term effect the war would have on British society.

insurance, subscriptions for war cemeteries and memorials or victory parades could allay their sense of injustice.

For ex-officers, the homecoming was even bleaker. On the assumption that they had 'connections' no provision was made for them at all. Not everyone had the stimulating war career of the second Duke of Westminster who in 1914 joined Sir John French's staff 'in an indeterminate position', arriving in a Rolls Royce car armed with a Hotchkiss machine-gun 'with which he succeeded in waging minor war on the enemy'. Neither did everyone have his assets, or his capacity to keep them. In the welter of taxes imposed in 1919 by a seemingly turncoat coalition government (the tergiversation of Conservative ministers was particularly painful) large numbers of landowners were forced to sell up. 'The old order is doomed', wrote the Duke of Marlborough in a letter to *The Times* on behalf of all those whose 'wealth is no longer fluid but is fixed in great houses and their surroundings', and in the name of social equality these 'fortresses of territorial influence will be razed to the ground'.

To some extent the Duke's Cassandra-like prophecies were fulfilled. The *Estates Gazette*

Ring in the New

28

In 1919 *Queen* complained that 'a month of the London season has gone by, but as yet none of the great houses have done any entertaining and compared to the seasons of pre-war days this one seems likely to be unimportant. Royal parties are few and far between, and there seems nothing to take the place of such great places of entertaining in the past as Devonshire House, Grosvenor House, and Montague House.' Despite the dissatisfactions of *Queen*, however, High Society in the early 1920s showed few superficial signs of the ravages of the war years. Mayfair was still full of mansions occupied by the families who had built them, and run by staffs of thirty or forty servants, and the country was still dotted with great houses staffed almost as generously as before. Grand households still boasted stewards, liveried footmen, butlers, chefs and chauffeurs, even if guests helped themselves to breakfast and no longer changed for tea. The *Queen* coyly categorized the gentility of the 'new poor', in which 'Lady Great House' had to 'shut down all but the best eight bedrooms (and four staff rooms) and to keep only a useful maid, a cook, a between maid, a parlour maid and a housemaid' and point out that 'Mrs Newly Rich', for all her money, did not aspire to an establishment such as that maintained by 'Lady Great House' before the war (only a housekeeper, three servants in the kitchen, three in the pantry, a houseboy and three housemaids). However Lord Lonsdale still managed to turn out his enormous staff in yellow livery and the Astors still had 'thirty indoor servants at Clivedon . . .exclusive of three dailies.'

Perhaps nothing could equal the reception

given by Lord Lonsdale for the Kaiser when he visited Lowther Castle in 1895. The royal visitor was escorted to the house by a procession consisting of Quorn Hunt servants in hunting kit, a squadron of Yeomanry, followed by

two outriders in blue coats preceding a dark phaeton in which were Lord Lonsdale and his brother Lancelot – about ten vehicles altogether in the cortege, each drawn by two chestnuts, driven postillion, with a footman up behind. All the servants were in Lonsdale livery of white breeches and waistcoat, yellow jacket with device on the left sleeve, and white beaver hats.

After a dinner for approximately seventy people he was entertained by Lord Lonsdale's private orchestra, under the direction of Mr James Hamilton, who had composed a special march for the guest of honour. Apart from the particular interest aroused by the Kaiser's presence, these arrangements were not at all unusual, nor did they stretch Lowther's abundant resources in the least. Sixty or seventy people dined there frequently and his yellow carriages were a common sight at Penrith station.

Conspicuous manifestations of opulence had always been a part of aristocratic life. Immense satisfaction was to be had in outdoing one's neighbours in the size and accoutrements of house and grounds. An outward show of wealth was by no means considered vulgar – on the contrary it was much admired. Queen Victoria, whose private estates totalled a mere 27,447 acres, marvelled at the ample domains of her richest subjects, notably in Scotland. In *Leaves from the Journal of Our Life in the Highlands* she remarked that from a vantage point on the Duke of

Previous page: The Old Berkshire Foxhounds meet at Beckett, Shrivenham, the seat of Viscount Barrington.

Below: A peaceful scene in London's Berkeley Square in April 1924.

Left: Park Lane, one of London's most prestigious streets in the heart of Mayfair.

Bottom left: Hyde Park, in the centre of London, provides a welcome breath of fresh air for strollers in 1919.

Below: A cartoon portrayal of the Prince of Wales.

Sutherland's estates 'We got a very extensive view, though not quite clear, of endless hills between this and the West coast – all the Duke's property – where the Westminsters have two, if not three, forests, of the Duke's.'

Certainly the Scottish dukes had a monopoly of land. The Duke of Sutherland owned 1,358,546 acres, of which 1,343,000 were in Scotland, and had at least five houses in Scotland and four, including the vast Italianate pile of Trentham, in England. It was said that when the Shah of Persia visited Trentham in 1873 he was overheard warning the Prince of Wales that the 'Duke of Sutherland is far too grand a subject – you'll have to have his head off when you come to the Throne . . .' His nearest rival, the Duke of Buccleuch, had his principal seat, Dalkeith Palace, near Edinburgh, but he also had Bowhill, a shooting lodge turned palace in Selkirkshire, Bransholme in Roxburgh, and Drumlanrig and Langholm Castles in Dumfriesshire, as well as Boughton House in Northamptonshire and Ditton Park in Buckinghamshire. Altogether he owned 458,739 acres, spread over thirteen counties.

Apart from land, castles and mansions, there were other criteria for measuring status: the distance one could march without treading on another man's land (about sixty miles for the Dukes of Sutherland and Buccleuch), the length of estate walls (Woburn twelve miles, Welbeck eight); the number of rooms (Knole 365); the number of usable guest rooms; the number of church livings in gift (the Duke of Devonshire had over forty); the possession of state apartments suitable for receiving visiting potentates; as well as the number of London houses, foreign villas and yachts.

Some went a stage further. The Duke of Atholl boasted a private army, the Atholl Highlanders, raised in 1839 to support the future sixth Duke at the Eglinton Tournament. The reclusive fifth Duke of Portland built a series of subterranean public rooms at Welbeck, reached by a mile-long drive carved out below the park, which included a ballroom (said to be the largest private apartment in England at 174 feet long, 64 feet wide and 22 feet high), a glass-roofed conservatory and a library 250 feet long. Food for this underground retreat was sent down from the kitchens in a heated truck, which ran on rails for 150 yards into the dining room, where it was kept hot in a steam-heated cupboard.

The upkeep of such grandiose establishments depended on an army of servants. Before the introduction of such modern comforts as hot running water, electricity and the motor car, watermen carried water up and down the stairs in buckets strung on yokes, housemaids swept and laid the grates, lamplighters lit the lamps and cooks managed to produce the vast amount of food needed to fuel both the idle and the working members of the household on a complex system of roasting ranges, stewing stoves, boiling stoves, turnspits and hot-closets.

Even after these improvements became comparatively commonplace, the very rich needed a considerable number of retainers to convert their vision of the way things should be into reality. The second Duke of Westminster, whose sudden moods and capricious demands tested his employees' resources to the limit, was one of the few who managed to keep up his flamboyant and extravagant way of life after the First World War. Described by Noel Coward as a man of 'notorious per-

sonal charm . . . who had he lived in an earlier age would undoubtedly have glittered with rhinestones from head to foot', he made few concessions to the post-war mood of auster-ity, except to transfer some of his assets to richer, newer countries, such as Australia and Canada. Eaton Hall and Bourdon House were kept fully staffed, as were his French chateaux and his two palatial yachts. 'Wherever he went', as one historian related, 'trains were held up for him and priority gangways were erected. His own couriers and courtiers met him everywhere to discharge his public and private errands. He hired bands, orchestras and entertainers as other men hired plumbers. Whenever he began a new courtship jewellers rejoiced.'

Opposite, top: Lord Lonsdale and Lady Juliet Duff enjoy a day at Kempton Park Races.

Opposite, bottom: A group of guests pictured on the terrace of Eaton Hall during one of the Duchess of Westminster's house parties.

Left: The third State Room at Boughton House, one of the Duke of Buccleuch's many properties. He owned 458,739 acres of land spread over 13 counties.

Below: The 2nd Duke of Westminster was an avid polo player and horse breeder.

Above: The 2nd Duke of Westminster playing polo at Hurlingham in a match between Eton and Hurlingham Clubs. The Duke's lifestyle continued in the grand manner after the war. Many of the landed gentry were adversely affected by taxation.

Right: Queen Mary was considered rather formal and old-fashioned, but won the love of her subjects during World War I by her devotion to duty and her adoption of rationing.

Not for him the little economies urged on its readers by *Queen*, who even went so far as to recommend living in Putney, an area previously considered unfit for upper-class habitation, excusing themselves on the grounds that although 'in former days, Putney, though possessed of many advantages could scarcely be classed as an aristocratic quarter, yet during part of the war a marquis lived and died there; and, even now, a well-known peeress is negotiating for quite a small dwelling...' It was a world far removed from Loelia, Duchess of Westminster, wife of the second Duke, whose main difficulty at the first party she gave at Eaton Hall after her marriage was to find her way round the house:

I got the hang of the ground-floor rooms quite easily, but the fifty-four bedrooms prepared for the guests defeated me ... everything was done to make things easy, but during that first house-party, after welcoming each arrival and glancing at the bedroom list, I had to ring for the butler to show me, as well as the visitors, up which particular staircase the Red Room or the Tower Room was located.

Other aristocrats, however, were content to live in simpler style. King George V and Queen Mary started off their married life as Duke and Duchess of York under less than princely conditions. York Cottage, on the Sandringham estate, was described by Princess Adelaide of Teck, Queen Mary's mother, as an 'ornate hutch', and while she admitted that it was an 'ideal cottage' she felt that it was far too small for their establishment and badly needed enlarging. In fact, the cottage, which stood, in the words of Queen Mary's biographer, James Pope-Hennessy, 'upon the brink of a reed-choked pond in one corner of the Sandringham deer park, some five minutes' walk from Sandringham House', had originally been designed to accommodate the overflow of bachelor guests from the big house and was not built for feminine convenience. Small and cramped, it was a maze of tiny rooms connected by narrow passages. It had been designed by a Colonel Edis, who was the Prince of Wales' favourite architect. Although Colonel Edis doubtless had much to recommend him, there was one drawback about employing him in the capacity in which the Prince had done: he was not really an architect at all. The result of this unusual commission was a mixture of influences. Tudor black and white mingled with Victorian Gothic, pebble-dash with rough-cast. Gables, hexagonal turrets, beams and tiny balconies clustered on the outside. 'It resembled', as James Pope Hennessy wrote, 'those improbable houses which children can concoct with a box of Swiss or German toy

Far left: George and Mary at Mar Lodge. They kept to a strict routine, going to Balmoral for the grouse season, Sandringham for Christmas and London for six months of official and social engagements.

Left: Loelia, Duchess of Westminster, led an extravagant social life. Everything was done in style; when she travelled trains were held up for her and an army of servants gratified her every whim.

Below: York Cottage, Sandringham, was the first home of George and Mary. Despite the cramped conditions they were very fond of the house.

K COTTAGE, SANDRINGHAM. B-1168

STEREOSCOPIC C°

Above: The White Drawing Room at Buckingham Palace. When Queen Mary moved to Buckingham Palace she found the distances between rooms quite exhausting.

Right: King George V and Queen Mary on an official visit to Liverpool Cathedral in 1924.

bricks.' It was every bit as peculiar inside. Unlike most country houses, where the kitchens and the servants' quarters were far removed from the main body of the house, the kitchens at York Cottage were in the basements, and the whole house 'reeked, before each meal, of food'. To crown it all there was an 'insufficient' number of baths.

Against all the odds, the Duke and Duchess adored their *bijou* residence. They lived in it for thirty three years, and were desolate when they had to move to Buckingham Palace. Queen Mary complained that it was strange and lonely and that she felt lost. 'Everything is so straggly, such distances to go and so fatiguing.' The King tried to restore her spirits by pointing out that the exercise would do her good, as she 'never walked a yard in London.' London, for the Duke and Duchess of York, had meant Marlborough House, and that, too, was compared favourably with their new home. 'Oh, how I regret our dear beloved Marlborough House', she wrote, 'the most perfect of all houses and so compact . . . Buckingham Palace is not so *gemutlich. . .*'

Gemutlichkeit (which roughly translated means cosiness) was something towards which the new King and Queen had strong leanings. King George V was of a reserved temperament, disliked entertaining and was naturally abstemious and Queen Mary, although possessing a healthy feminine liking for clothes, was bored by the hours it was necessary to spend with dressmakers and milliners. As a result, their public image was not flattering. Loelia, Duchess of Westminster wrote in her memoirs when King George and Queen Mary first came to the throne:

They were considered so stuffy and frumpish that they were very much sneered at behind their backs. Any funny story that depended for its effect on being told about very prudish people was pinned on them . . . Rude poems were circulated, like the one by Max Beerbohm, each verse of which ends either "The King is duller than the Queen" or "The Queen is duller than the King".

These unkind comments were muffled during the war, and after it was over the qualities of stoicism, diligence and sobriety that the King and Queen had displayed and the high example they had set in adopting rationing and renouncing alcoholic drink in all the Royal residences during the food shortages of 1917, produced a genuinely grateful and affectionate response. They might be old-fashioined, quiet and formal, but they symbolized stability and standards in a disintegrating world.

Stability and standards, combined with a romantic attachment to the past became, however, a sign of middle age. Younger members of society were not at all inhibited by lack of money, or by declining standards of living. Lady Diana Cooper, the youngest daughter of the Duke of Rutland, spent much of her childhood at Belvoir Castle and came out in 1911, Coronation Year. On 27 June 1919 she married Duff Cooper, then a clerk in the Foreign Office, at St. Margaret's, Westminster, amid scenes of great excitement. 'There were wedding crowds surging as there are today in Parliament Square, and the wedding bells were crashing, and fatherly mounted police were imperceptibly controlling the jolly riot' wrote Lady Diana. 'My mother was smiling. That day had no shadow.'

All obstacles had by then been eliminated, but beforehand there had been a number of objections raised by the Duke and Duchess. How would their beautiful, talented and celebrated daughter manage as the wife of a penniless Foreign Office clerk? They had only £1200 between them. As Duff Cooper himself remarked: 'The least worldly of parents would have been justified in hoping that she would marry somebody whose great name, whose vast possessions or whose splendid achievements would seem to justify her choice. I had none of those things, nor any prospect of acquiring them.'

Her parents need not have worried.

Above: Queen Mary's Sitting Room (The Boudoir) in Marlborough House, her London home before Buckingham Palace. She found it cosy and comfortable, and compared it favourably with the Palace.

Above: One of Chanel's exquisite dress designs. She supplied Lady Diana Cooper with outfits free of charge.

Below: The Devon and Somerset Hounds, August 1926.

Cocooned by adoring friends, who showered them with cheques, jewels, furniture, gold plate, silver, clocks, chandeliers, carpets, mirrors, wine and even (from Lord Beaverbrook) a motor car, the gilded pair drifted across Europe in a haze of magnificence. Sir Philip Sassoon lent them his exotic house at Lympne, they stayed at the Ritz Hotel in Paris, at I Tatti in Florence, at the Grand Hotel in Rome (a present from Marconi) and at Lord Grimthorpe's Villa Cimbrone high in the mountains above Ravello.

Soon after they returned to England, they rented a house in Gower Street. By this time the Duchess, who had begun to see that a 'daughter dependent and poor gave her more scope for help and invention than the others who lived secure in their married estates', had unbent completely. With a practical enthusiasm that would have been unheard of five years before, she climbed up a ladder in the bathroom and helped her daughter paint trees, birds and butterflies on the walls, a design taken from a Chinese paper at Belvoir.

The house itself was a far cry from Arlington Street, the site of the Duchess's London Mansion. ('What a quarter, Violet, what a quarter' exclaimed her friend, Lady Scarborough, raising her hands in horror.) There was a hall, an upstairs drawing-room, a library, a dining room, two bedrooms and a bathroom and, on the top floor, rooms for the servants. They could only afford what Lady Diana described as the bare minimum of staff, 'five for the two of us', (a lady's maid, a manservant, a housemaid, a cook and a 'tweeny', or maid of all work). It all seemed to bear out the *Queen*'s predictions for 'Lady Great House' to an alarming degree.

The *Queen*, however, had not allowed for enterprise and discrimination. Transformed by *objets de vertu* and carpeted in white, the house reflected the taste of its occupants; it was both a monument to the past and a gesture of optimism for the future. No dingy, mousy acceptance of genteel poverty here,

but an inventive and colourful victory over the prophets of doom. To it came a stream of visitors including Winston Churchill, Lord Beaverbrook, Edwin Montagu, Maurice Baring, Iris Tree, Ethel Smythe and Hilaire Belloc. Chaliapin brought a Russian quartet of male singers and they sang in a garden 'magically transformed by light and laughter into a poor man's Parnassus'.

Although they lived above their means they were never in debt. Lady Diana admitted that this was largely due to 'a reconciled and loving family, good friends, treats, foreign holidays' (when they gambled successfully at chemin-de-fer) and 'dressing without bills' (Ospovat, Molyneux, Chanel and Patou were faithful accolytes), but supplementing their income was never far from their minds. Duff took to part-time journalism for the *Daily Express*, his wife looked covetously across the Atlantic to Hollywood. 'I suppose' said the social editress of the *Daily Express* in Evelyn Waugh's *Vile Bodies*, 'you don't know of anyone who'd care to take on the job?' 'What do they pay?' asked Adam Fenwick-Symes. 'Ten pounds a week and expenses.' 'I'd do it myself for that', said Adam.

Earning money by the sweat of one's brow instead of acquiring it by divine right was one of the new inconveniences that the upper classes had to contend with after the war. The *Queen* explored the economic possibilities of rabbit breeding, bee keeping and basket making. Ladies of fashion who could afford it started up boutiques or magazines. Impecunious young men took jobs as private secretaries to cigar-smoking millionaires or tried to marry American heiresses.

The early novels of P G Wodehouse are studded with such characters. Bertie Wooster's foxhunting Aunt Dahlia started a magazine, *Milady's Boudoir*, and Bertie contributed the odd article on 'What the well Dressed Man is wearing'. Old Etonian Berry Conway became secretary to the unscrupulous and dispeptic American financier T Paterson Frisby, after his rich aunt 'suddenly turned into a poor aunt'. T Paterson's heiress niece was chaperoned during the London Season by Berry's old schoolfriend's aunt, Lady Vera Hoddesdon, for a fee of two thousand pounds. Her nephew, Lord Biskerton, became engaged to the heiress, who succumbed not so much to him as to the crumbling charms of his ancestral seat. As he pointed out to his father, the Earl of Hoddesdon, 'it costs a fortune to keep up and it's too big to let and a white elephant generally, but there's one thing about it – it's romantic. . . . There isn't a girl in the world who could have held out in a setting like that.' The Earl, jubilant at the prospect of money in the bank, could only agree.

At least in fiction the son and heir was saved from penury by the ample resources of his fiancée. In fact, the grandson of the eleventh Duke of Bedford had more difficulty solving his pressing financial problems. Despite his grandfather's enormous wealth (it was said of his predecessor that he could throw £200,000 a year into the Thames and still keep Woburn) as a young man about town in 1936 he had to make do on an allowance of ninety eight pounds a year and, when he married at the age of twenty one against his grandfather's wishes, he was cut off without a penny and was obliged to take a job in an estate agents. The old Duke and his deaf Duchess sat in solitary state at Woburn, which was kept up with full Victorian solemnity; an endless retinue of servants (fifty indoor and two hundred outdoor) pandering to their every need. Two houses in Belgrave Square lay fully staffed and idle, while in Bloomsbury his grandson lodged in a boarding house for overseas students. When he finally inherited, in 1953, the unsettled estate was valued at £802,252 and the settled lands valued at £7,800,000, which qualified for £4,500,000 in tax. Lord Biskerton said:

The fact of the matter is, laddie, there's nothing in being an Earl nowadays. It's a mug's game. . . . What with the Land Tax, and the Income Tax and the Super Tax and all the rest of the little Taxes, there's not much in the family sock these days . . . It all comes down to this. If England wants a happy, well-fed aristocracy, she mustn't have wars. She can't have it both ways.

The thirteenth Duke of Bedford could hardly have put it better.

Above: Lady Diana Cooper managed to live in a grand style despite a constant shortage of money, and attracted a stream of visitors to her house in Gower Street.

Below: Duff Cooper was a poor clerk in the foreign office when he married Diana, and had to resort to journalism to supplement his income.

The Younger Set

'I see', wrote King George V to Queen Mary in 1925, 'David continues to dance every night . . . people who don't know will begin to think that either he is mad or the biggest rake in Europe. Such a pity.' King George was not alone in casting a disapproving eye over his firstborn. London was full of soberly-brought-up elders raging against the insouciance and lack of respect displayed by the youngsters. The younger generation was a constant topic of conversation; their escapades, their parties, their clothes, their morals, all excited extreme interest and censor. 'I don't understand them and I don't want to', said Mr Outrage, in *Vile Bodies*, 'They had a chance after the war that no generation has ever had. There was a whole civilisation to be saved and remade – and all they seem to do is to play the fool.'

Playing the fool in all its diverting guises had never been more fun. Gone were the stuffy conventions and hidebound rules that had governed polite society before the war. Carefully arranged piled-up hair, hour-glass figures, whalebone corsets, wine-cup and the waltz had been replaced by the bob, loose clothes, dry martinis, the tango and the shimmy-shake. Young men and women danced together cheek to cheek with shameless abandon, women were seen smoking Egyptian and Turkish cigarettes through long ivory holders, or driving themselves in smart open-air roadsters, small, round felt hats pulled down over their eyes.

Previous page: Race-goers view the meeting from the top of a coach at one of the highspots of the sporting season – Ascot.

Above right: A cartoon from *The Illustrated London News.* The original caption reads: "'ENTR'ACTE': White-tie and black chiffon and georgette discuss tennis, drinks, cigarettes, polo, books, cricket, opera, dancing, cigars, food, wine, enemies, friends scandals and, possibly, the play."

Below: Pyjama suits were fashion news in 1928. This model is casually smoking a long cigarette, which would have caused a scandal before the war.

The hero of Michael Arlen's fanciful and verbose novel, *The Green Hat*, first published in 1924, looked out of his rooms in Shepherd's Market one night to see just such a lady standing outside his front door. Parked by the side of the road was a:

long, low yellow car which shone like a battle chariot. . . . Open as a yacht, it wore a great shining bonnet, and flying over the crest of this great bonnet, as though in proud flight over the heads of scores of phantom horses, was that silver stork by which the gentle may be pleased to know that they have just escaped death beneath the wheels of a Hispano-Suiza car . . .

His visitor was 'tall, not very tall, but as tall as becomes a woman' and she was wearing a green felt hat, 'one of those that women who have many hats affect pour le sport' and a lighter leather jacket (also pour le sport) which had a 'high collar of the fur of a few minks'. Her name was Iris Storm.

The story of Iris Storm touched a chord in the hearts of the most hard-bitten Bright Young Thing. There wasn't a girl in the land who didn't identify with her mysterious beauty, her troubled past and her doomed future. They yearned for her immaculately shingled auburn hair, for her small, white face and her silky red mouth. They worshipped her intensity, her helpless nymphomania, her desire to die for purity. When, in the end, she drove her Hispano-Suiza into a tree at seventy one miles an hour, they admired the reckless manner of her death.

In real life, the Hon Mrs Dudley Ward ran her a near second. Described as a 'dark-eyed beauty, with sleek short hair, a slim figure and a rather wistful air of melancholy, which

besides giving her a most alluring quality encouraged men to feel protective towards her', she was seen frequently at the Embassy Club in Bond Street, dancing with the Prince of Wales and his boon companions, 'Fruity' Metcalfe (married to Lord Curzon's daughter), 'Burghie' (the Earl of Westmorland) and 'Dickie' Mountbatten (married to Edwina Ashley, Sir Ernest Cassell's granddaughter). Her looks, her clothes and her seductive penchant for winding snake bracelets up her arms were slavishly copied. She had only to appear once in a backless dress with her eyes darkened at the rims for a hundred bare-backed, kohl-rimmed hopefuls to follow in her wake.

The merry-go-round of pleasure enjoyed by the Prince of Wales and his friends revolved, as it had always done, around the London Season. Unlike his father, however, whose seasonal migrations were 'as regular as the revolving planets' and which included Sandringham in January, London in February for six months of official and social engagements (with visits to Windsor for Easter and Ascot), Newmarket for the Jockey Club race meetings, Goodwood, Cowes, Balmoral for the grouse shooting and the deer stalking, London again in October, interspersed by journeys to Sandringham (for the partridge and pheasant shoots) and, finally, the family gathering there at Christmas – the Prince preferred a more flexible régime.

Both his parents watched with barely concealed impatience while their errant son slip-

Above: Miss Betty Blythe, famous screen beauty, dancing the tango with the principal of the Park Lane Dancing School, 1925.

Left: The West Kent Hounds meet at Penhurst Station in a less traditional vehicle.

42

Above: A couple enjoy a quiet moment at the Marlow Regatta, June 1923.

Right: A typical scene from the Henley Regatta in July 1926.

Below: A view of the six-metre race at the Cowes Regatta, one of the most important sporting events of the Season.

ped away from the guns during the shooting season at Sandringham in order to play golf, or risked his neck in foolhardy attempts to win at steeplechasing. They shook their heads over disquieting rumours that, on his travels around the world, he sometimes took 'evasive action when confronted with the wives of the officials at Government House, preferring to dance with girls of his own age, or to disappear altogether. . .with his young cousin "Dickie" Mountbatten.' Other exploits, such as leaping onto the back of a bucking bronco at Saskatoon, and riding it around the ring to the accompaniment of the 'ecstatic applause of the assembled crowds' or allowing himself to be photographed bathing, caused his father, in particular, to reflect mournfully on how very different it had all been when he and Queen Mary had visited India as Prince and Princess of Wales in 1905.

The Younger Generation, on the other hand, were in raptures. Here at last was a figurehead worthy of their attention and respect, able to bend the straitlaced round of formal dances, race meetings, regattas and country house visits that made up the Season to his will. Galloping in his wake they evaded their chaperones and swarmed into the newly formed and daringly unrespectable nightclubs, into the Cavendish Hotel, where Rosa Lewis welcomed them with open arms, and into the Savoy Hotel, where they could dance the Twinkle, the Jog Trot or the Vampire in between sipping China tea and eating cucumber sandwiches. It was all heavenly fun.

The Nightclub was a phenomenon that sprang from the restrictions in licensing laws during the war and their reputations varied considerably. The most fashionable were the Night Light, which had two princesses and four peers on its committee, the Kit-Kat and the Embassy which were both patronized by the Prince of Wales. Less reputable was the 43 Club in Gerrard Street, founded by Mrs Kate Meyrick. Although her visitors' list was distinguished – it included the Crown Prince of Sweden, Prince Nicholas of Rumania, Michael Arlen, and Jimmy White, the Lancashire millionaire who one night brought six Daimlers full of showgirls and ran a champagne party that cost £400 – she maintained an uneasy relationship with the police. The police in any case tended to raid all nightclubs on principle, in the hope of uncovering illegal drinking, or some equally nefarious crime. (They even went so far as to raid the Kit-Kat, on a night after the Prince of Wales had been there, but with little result, except to frighten away a few débutantes for a night or two.)

As far as the 43 Club went, they had some grounds for suspicion. Mrs Meyrick was a lady of energy and resource, whose three daughters all married into the peerage (to Lord Kinnoull, the racing motorist, Lord de Clifford and the Earl of Craven). Her other establishments included the Manhatten, patronized by Sophie Tucker and Rudolph Valentino, and the Silver Slipper in Regent Street, which had a dance-floor made of glass. The 43 Club was not without its problems,

Above: The crowded river at the 1932 Henley Regatta. The Regatta regained its popularity in the 1930s.

Left: A rather luxurious picnic at the Derby in 1929.

ASCOT: 1931
A Survey of the Fashions that have Created a Stir

THE ART OF THE FLOUNCE: A picture gown in tiers of ecru lace

ONE—TWO—THREE: Lord Glanely's Grand Salute, Mr. Esmond's Ellenborough, and the Dowager Lady Nunburnholme's Racedale in the unsaddling enclosure after the Royal Hunt Cup

A PYJAMA MODE: An unusual creation in flimsy flounced georgette and sable velvet

A QUASI-VICTORIAN FASHION: A striking creation in parchment taffeta worn with a picture hat to match

CHEQUERBOARD: Miss E. G. Elsock enjoys a puff of a cigarette. The short-waisted jacket is quite Victorian

FIGURES OF THE STAGE: Mr. Edgar Wallace and Lady Lindsay Hogg (Frances Doble). The latter wears a fetching creation in muslin and lace eminently cool and refreshing to behold

THE CARTWHEEL HAT worn above a flounced frock, shrouded in a dust-coat, was popular at 1931 Ascot

THE PICNIC: Many Ascot parties elect to take a collation with them and enjoy (weather permitting) an alfresco meal on the course. Cold chicken, strawberries, and champagne (the staples of Ascot) go well on the top of a coach or on a trestle table

LONG SKIRT AND BOLERO: The athletic figure of 1931 looks very novel in the modes deriving from past eras

SHEERNESS OF LINE: Miss Cellinette in an ensemble of black and white. The ankle-length skirt seemed short amid the ground-trailers that were to be seen on every side, although not so brief as others

"THE GLASS OF FASHION AND THE MOULD OF FORM": Three examples of the cycle which fashion has performed, having swung full circle from Victorianism through the abbreviated modes of the past decade back to the long skirt and picture hats of 1931. Umbrellas were an essential this year

LONG, LONGER, LONGEST: A study of the modern skirt. That on the right would have been considered very hampering a couple of years ago, but to-day it is definitely short. The central figure recalls the fichu of Victorian days, while on left is a flowered creation. With the increase in length of skirts, there is a corresponding enlargement of the hat

SHELTERING FROM THE UBIQUITOUS RAIN: Miss Nisbet, in a flowered "daisy cotton," on the long lawns of to-day have been termed by the wits. The umbrella is an essential if any smart woman is to remain smart this summer

Above: Ascot was, and still is, an occasion to display new fashions, particularly in hats.

however. 'Brilliant' Chang, the dope smuggler, was a member, and ran his operations from the club, and although she claimed repeatedly that she had tried to stop him peddling his wares from her premises, she was continuously harassed by the police. In 1924 they finally managed to pin her down and, amid cries of protest from her admirers, who remained staunchly devoted to her, she was sent to Holloway for six months. Later, in 1928, she was sent to prison again, this time for fifteen months, after she had been accused of receiving false money. None of these setbacks, however, daunted her in the least. When she came out of prison in 1930 she went on a Continental tour and then, as Robert Graves commented, 'carried on the "43", adding Jim Mollison, the airman, and Primo Carnera, the Boxer, to her roll of honour, but taking no risks with the police.'

Rosa Lewis, the proprietress of the Cavendish Hotel, ran an altogether different establishment. Immortalized by Evelyn Waugh as Lottie Crump in *Vile Bodies* (a characterization which infuriated her) she provided a refuge and a relaxation for countless raffish aristocrats. The fifth child of a watchmaker, she went into domestic service at the age of

twelve. When she was sixteen she went to work for the Comte and Comtesse de Paris as an under-kitchen maid. By the time she was twenty she was cooking for Lady Randolph Churchill, and four years later was a successful freelance, producing meals in the grand manner for King Edward VII and his set. She acquired the Cavendish in 1902, furnishing the rooms in the style of the large country houses in which she had worked and maintaining a discreet silence if any of them were put to a more intimate use than that of drinking and sleeping. Not surprisingly it became very popular. A hotel which combined the privacy of a club, the pleasures of an endless house-party in full swing and the fantasies of Elinor Glyn, and which was within walking distance of Buckingham Palace, the best clubs and the most fashionable shops was bound to be pounced on by the racier members of Society.

When war broke out, Rosa, like Lottie Crump, 'took down the photograph of the Kaiser and, with some solemnity, hung it in the manservants' lavatory.' Like Lottie, too, she had her worries after it was over: 'income-tax forms and drink restrictions and young men whose fathers she used to know, who give her bad cheques . . .' But these troubles were soon forgotten. One could still go to the Cavendish, as one could to Shepherd's Hotel, 'parched with modernity' and if Rosa liked your face 'draw up, cool and uncontaminated, great healing draughts from the well of Edwardian certainty.'

During the 1920s, on summer nights in between dances, the sons and daughters of her favourite Edwardian clients, hungry for cheap champagne and the fun of Rosa's licentious tongue, would pile into taxis and set out for the Cavendish. Nancy Mitford, Daphne Vivian (later the Marchioness of Bath), Elizabeth Ponsonby, Lettice Lygon (Lord Beauchamp's daughter) David and Olivia Plunket-Greene, Brian Howard – all injected new life into the fading red plush and morocco and perpetuated the convenient myth that nothing in the social order had changed in the least.

Some things, indeed, had not. To make sure of meeting the right people at the right dances, and even at the right nightclubs, these social butterflies had to emerge from their chrysalises in an acceptable manner. Loelia, Duchess of Westminster, wrote:

That nebulous thing called London Society was larger than it had been before the war, but it was still exclusive and difficult for outsiders to enter. But once a nouveau riche was in she stayed in, and her children were completely assimilated. People gave dances for their daughters and the daughters of their old friends and, if one did not get married,

Above: Kate Meyrick *(centre)*, founder of the 43 Club which had a rather unsavoury reputation despite being patronized by many distinguished visitors.

one went on being asked to dances for years, perhaps enjoying each Season more than the last. The hostesses had to scrape round slightly to get enough men, but one way or another, there were enough regular dance-goers for two or three "good" dances to be possible on one night; we used to nip from dance to dance meeting . . . our friends.

Giving a dance in her daughter's honour to signify her arrival at a suitably emancipated age (usually eighteen) was the first step a

Left: An evocative photograph of débutantes by Cecil Beaton.

Right: Fancy dress balls were all the rage in the 1920s, and the wealthy went to enormous lengths to appear in stunning costumes. This photograph shows Mlle Nina Payne in Egyptian garb, April 1923.

Below: The Savoy Orpheans entertain guests and visitors at the Savoy Hotel in London. Hotels in the 1920s and 1930s offered many entertainments to entice the rich.

mother had to take to launch her in Society; the second and infinitely more important one was to ensure her presentation at Court. Court presentations, which had been suspended during the war and only restarted in 1920, remained rigidly conventional. Each débutante had to have a sponsor, known to the King and Queen, and no divorced person was acceptable. She was required to wear a train, which before the war had to be exactly three yards long and after the war, in the interests of economy, not more than eighteen inches. Also compulsory was a headdress made of a wisp of tulle and ostrich feathers – three for a débutante and two for a married lady.

Unless they had been given a privilege called the Éntree, or the right to enter the Palace by a side door, débutantes and their sponsors had to queue, often for more than three hours, first in the Mall and then outside the Throne Room, nervously awaiting the moment when they would be allowed to enter. In June 1920, when the first daylight Courts were held *The Times* recorded that the Mall was 'jammed with large black cars carrying débutantes in tiaras', remarking severely that 'one girl was noticed smoking a cigarette.'

As for the ceremony itself, it was over very quickly. As Loelia Ponsonby (later Duchess of Westminster) wrote, '[It] was over in a flash. One reached the head of the queue, handed one's invitation card to a splendid official, he shouted aloud one's name and tossed the card into a rather common-looking little waste paper basket, one advanced along the red carpet, stopped and made two curtsies to the King and Queen, who were sitting on a low dais surrounded by numerous relations, and then walked on.' This ordeal safely behind her, a débutante could settle down to enjoy herself and begin the serious business of capturing the hearts of those terrifying and elusive creatures – young men.

For at the forefront of every scheming mother's mind was the hope that her daughter would marry well and soon. Docile, well-behaved girls who lived up to their mother's expectations were judged pearls without price, but those who balked at the marriage market, or who took an independent line on whom they associated with were considered fast and difficult. Like the Duchess of Stayle, in *Vile Bodies*, they exerted considerable pressure on their daughters to accept any decent proposal of marriage, whether or not it was an obvious love-match. 'I think you'd better marry Edward', said the Duchess. 'But

Mama I don't want to ... I couldn't ... it would kill me.' The Duchess was adamant. 'You know your father and I only want your happiness, dear one ... Papa shall see Edward in the morning and make everything alright.'

Poor Lady Ursula married Edward Throbbing partly because she was unable or unwilling to stand up to her mother and partly because in the long run there were not enough young men to go round, and anything was better than nothing at all – and, anyway, it was better not to think too much about it. Trying not to think too much was important. Better not, when things looked so uncertain. If one allowed one's mind to dwell on the disturbances beneath the surface, the brittle exterior might crack, and what would happen then? One might come face to face with unemployment or poverty and might, like the Labour Party's doom-laden manifesto of 1920, begin to feel that 'the industrialist system of capitalist production ... with the monstrous inequality of circumstances which it produces and the degradation and brutalisation, both moral and spiritual resulting therefrom' had indeed been dealt a death blow. It was quite a relief to have the Conservatives in power again in 1924, but it did not seem to stop those annoying cries from The *Daily*

Herald, cheering on the lower classes and urging them to rise up and strike for freedom, and not to put up with lower pay for longer hours a minute longer. Far better to forget about the whole thing and go to a party.

In 1924 the *Daily Mail* noted, 'A New Society Game. Chasing Clues. Midnight Chase in London'. No doubt they had spotted Lady Eleanor Smith (daughter of the Earl of

Above: Débutantes learn the correct and incorrect way of picking up a handkerchief at a School for Manners in Kensington.

Below: Débutantes at Queen Charlotte's Birthday Ball, May 1931.

Birkenhead), Loelia Ponsonby and Zita and Theresa (Baby) Jungman and others haring about in their cars in the middle of the night, on one of their glorious Treasure Hunts. They had heard of the larks they had got up to – the screeching tyres in the forecourt of Buckingham Palace, the search for clues in sentry boxes, at the top of the Monument, at the foot of Queen Victoria's memorial, or somewhere daring in the East End. These ladies were, in any case, not unknown to them. They had already recorded their dazzlingly successful hoaxes: the one where Lady Eleanor had cards printed for 'Miss Babington Gooch, Amalgamated Provincial Press' and interviewed various celebrities staying at the Savoy and Claridges; and the one where Zita and Theresa dressed up as important foreigners and paid calls on total strangers – and felt they richly deserved to be dubbed Bright Young People.

Their parties, too, showed them to be wonderfully emancipated and original. So clever of Loelia Ponsonby and her brother to think of asking their friends to bring food and drink to St James Palace when their parents were away shooting and they felt like a party but had no money. It all went wonderfully well – Michael Arlen brought a case of pink champagne and Oliver Messel gave a one-man cabaret show. The newspapers were delighted; the Bright Young Things were at it again, and they were being even more wicked than usual - this time they were having a Bottle Party.

'Oh Nina', said Adam Fenwick-Symes, 'What a lot of parties' (Masked parties, Savage parties, Victorian parties, Greek parties, Wild West parties, Russian parties, Circus parties, parties where one had to dress as somebody else, almost naked parties in St John's Wood,

parties in flats and studios and houses and ships and hotels and night clubs, in windmills and swimming baths . . . dull dances in London and comic dances in Scotland and disgusting dances in Paris. . .)

Dressing-up was a pre-occupation indulged in with passionate attention to detail. When the Duchess of Sutherland gave a Baby party in 1927, Lord Portarlington and his son turned up dressed as a Victorian Dowager and her daughter, 'no hideous detail omitted', the Prince of Wales and the Duke of Kent went as little boys and Lord Ednam got himself up as a Nanny and wheeled Lady Ednam 'wearing a dreadful baby mask' about in a pram. At the Duchess's 1926 ball eight 'fashionable and elegant' ladies went as the Eton College Rowing Eight. 'They brought their boat with them', said Loelia Ponsonby, 'and, coxed by Mr Duff Cooper, rowed themselves into the ballroom.' At another dance in the same year Lady Oxford dressed up as an Indian gentleman with great effect – she asked to be introduced to Lord Birkenhead and he failed to recognize her, so completely had she immersed herself in the part.

On 30 April 1926 Lady Oxford and her daughter, Elizabeth Bibesco, went to the opening of the Summer Exhibition at the Royal Academy. Neither they nor the other celebrated guests who attended this, the first social event of the Season, appeared to have any intimations of the crisis that was to engulf the country within a matter of days. Far more interesting was the controversy that had broken out concerning one of the exhibits, a painting by Mr John B Souter, which depicted a nude woman dancing to a saxophone played by a negro and which the Colonial Office had demanded should be removed from the walls.

One or two of the more thoughtful members of Society had the odd premonition. Loelia Ponsonby recorded in her diary that she wondered if the country was on the brink of a bloody revolution, but hastily reminded herself that 'it was a possibility that had been at the back of the minds of the upper classes ever since the days of Marie Antoinette, and which they had got quite used to, so in the next sentence I went on to describe how I was trimming a hat or arranging a dinner party.'

The General Strike, when it came, was tremendous fun. Duff Cooper admitted to having 'a feeling of sick anxiety' and Lady Diana to hearing 'the tumbrils rolling and heads sneezing into the baskets' but on the whole Society found it all immensely exhilarating. 'Quite frankly', wrote Loelia Ponsonby, 'my friends and I were amused by the novelty and excitement of the strike and it was over before it had time to pall.' Strike stories abounded: who had driven what lorry, what train, manned which switchboard. Mrs

Richard Norton operated the switchboard of the *Daily Express*, Lady Diana Cooper 'sat up all night folding an abbreviated version of copies of *The Times*.'

After ten days it was all over. The *Daily Mail*'s headlines were 'Surrender of the Revolutionaries' and 'A Triumph for the People'. In Mayfair, attention turned to the marriage of the nineteen-year-old Lord de Clifford and Mrs Kate Meyrick's daughter Dorothy, and to the fancy dress party to be given by the Duchess of Sutherland at Hampden House, Green Street, W1, on 16 July.

'I'm told they're having another of their parties', said Mrs Mouse to her friend, Kitty (in *Vile Bodies*), 'in an aeroplane this time.'
'In an aeroplane? How very extraordinary.'
'What I always wonder, Kitty dear, is what they actually DO at these parties of theirs, I mean, do they. . .?'
'My dear, from all I hear, I think they do.'
'Oh, to be young again, Kitty. When I think, my dear, of all the trouble and exertion which we had to go through to be even moderately bad. . .'
'And yet, my dear, I doubt very much whether they really *appreciate* it all as much as we should . . . young people take things so much for granted. Si la jewnesse savait.'
'Si la vieillesse pouvait, Kitty.'

Social
Lionesses

Just before Kenneth Clark became Director of the National Gallery in 1933 he found that, unaccountably, he and his wife were 'borne along on the crest of a social wave'. They were asked everywhere and 'almost everyone of note' came to lunch or dinner with them. He could find no satisfactory explanation for this phenomenon, which lasted from 1932 until 1939, for, although, as Clark himself modestly admitted:

. . . we were quite presentable, there were far more handsome couples. We were comfortably off, but far richer people were trying to make their way into society, in vain. Our home contained some good pictures by artists who have since become fashionable – Cézanne, Renoir, Seurat, Matisse and Bonnard – which we had been able to buy at modest prices; but the high-powered people who visited us (other than Americans) never noticed them.

The best he could do was to compare their strange rise with the mysterious fluctuations of the Stock Exchange, for it was as inexplicable as a 'boom in Australian gold shares . . . and had as little to do with talent as Australian gold shares have to do with the precious metal in a mine.' It was not, however, quite as inex-

plicable as all that. Shares, like social fortunes, needed brokers to monitor their ups and downs. The brokers that kept an eye on social values were the hostesses. They could make or break a person's reputation.

In 1930, after reading Cecil Beaton's *Book of Beauty*, Lady Cunard was so outraged that she threw it on the fire. Her luncheon guests, according to Cecil Beaton, 'were astonished to watch her thrusting a poker through the burning covers, as she exclaimed in a high canary squeak, "He calls me a hostess, that shows he's a low fellow".' Whatever unflattering connotations the word 'hostess' brought to Lady Cunard's mind – probably some vision of a Clarissa Dalloway, shallow and self-absorbed, escorting her Prime Minister 'down the room, prancing, sparkling . . . having that gift still; to be; to exist; . . . all with the most perfect ease and air of a creature floating in its element . . .' – the fact remained that Lady Cunard would be remembered, not for her tiny waist, nor for her musical gifts nor for her alert and original mind, but for her extraordinary ability to hypnotize a roomful of ill-assorted celebrities into leaning towards her as sunflowers bend towards the sun, in united recognition of her life-giving force; in short, her skill as a hostess.

It was not a pursuit for the fainthearted. Strong nerves, physical stamina and a taste for intrigue were important, a determination to succeed and a rich, acquiescent and preferably absent husband a necessity. Apart from their financial assets, husbands were not objects greatly prized by society hostesses. Lovers, or at the very least, a respectable quota of passionate admirers, were far more desirable. Unlike husbands, who more often than not droned on about their jobs in the city or their country pursuits, lovers could be relied upon to have similar interests and, if they were important enough, to add colour and stature both to the object of his affection and to her salon. For a salon was what these indomitable ladies were struggling to create, whether it was political, royal or just competing for the attentions of the literary artistic lions of the moment.

The political salon, which in its heyday produced an atmosphere (remembered by Somerset Maugham) in which a hostess could say to a Prime Minister, 'We're agreed, then, that Freddie shall have India', was, during the 1920s and 1930s, dominated by Lady Londonderry. Her principal rivals, Lady Londesborough, Lady Ribblesdale, Lady Astor, Lady Wimborne and Mrs Greville, all had points in their favour but none pursued her goal with as much panache. Born Edith Chaplin, a granddaughter of the third Duke of Sutherland, Lady Londonderry married Charles Steward Henry Vane-Tempest-

Previous page: Lady Londonderry, who dominated the political salons in the 1920s and 1930s, seen with Victor Halcolm at a ball in Grosvenor House.

Below: The Marchioness of Londonderry, suitably dressed to receive the King and Queen at her London home in 1927.

Left: Lady Ribblesdale, one of Lady Londonderry's chief rivals, at the Lawn Tennis Tournament at Hanover Lodge, Regent's Park, June 1923.

Below: Kenneth Clark with his family in 1934. Somewhat to his surprise, he found himself a much sought-after guest with society hostesses.

54

Above: Lady Astor opening a maternity home in Plymouth, June 1923. As well as being a renowned hostess she was known for her interest in social problems.

Stewart in 1899. In 1903, after a near fatal illness, she went on a convalescent trip to the Far East and while in Japan had one of her legs tattooed with a snake pattern. During the war, in between running a hospital at Londonderry House and founding the Women's Legion, she started a society called The Ark. Its members, all of whom were given the name of a bird or a beast or a mythological creature, met regularly at Londonderry House in order to discuss politics or exchange the news of the day. Each name was considered to be both significant and apposite – Lady Londonderry herself was christened 'Circe and Sorceress', her husband became 'Charlie the Cheetah', Winston Churchill, 'Winston the Warlock' and Ramsay MacDonald, 'Hamish the Hart'.

Ramsay MacDonald fell into the category of passionate admirer. They met in 1924 at a dinner given by the King and Queen in his honour, when he, as the new Prime Minister, was asked to take Lady Londonderry in to dinner. They took to each other at once, finding a common bond in the Scottish High-

lands and Gaelic folk-lore, to which they were both devoted. Visits to Chequers were soon arranged, and a regular correspondence on matters of political interest followed. In 1929, after he was returned to power in a minority government, Lady Londonderry asked him to join her Ark Society, and invited him to call her by her Ark name, 'Circe'.

'The invitation to enter your Ark delights me', he wrote from 10 Downing Street, 'What ponderings it awakens! Am I to escape the flood which is sure to come upon this ungodly nation? What am I to be? – a bear? a serpent? a wolf (in sheep's clothing or not)? a lamb? What?' His title met with his approval, but he could not bring himself to call Lady Londonderry 'Circe'. It did not seem right for a Tory hostess, or for someone so statuesquely beautiful. She should be the glorious huntress, Diana. He wrote:

Nay, nay, surely not Circe. Was she not a wicked witch? Witches I love. But they should be good and romantic, and of the family of that delightful creature Diana . . . I want walks with someone who can smile and blush – to wit, Diana. But

Circe! Circe is uncanny. Circe's mother was met by Macbeth. Circe cannot dance, Circe cannot sing, Circe has no quaint humours. Circe belongs to the Devils who were never in Heaven . . .

Despite his obviously slavish devotion – he succumbed to 'Circe' and wrote to her at least once a week, addressing her as 'my dear Ladye', 'My dear' or 'My dear one' – Ramsay MacDonald became something of a thorn in Lady Londonderry's flesh. While enjoying to the full his attentions and feeling it only her natural right to have him, when Prime Minister, standing at her side at the top of the dramatic staircase of Londonderry House at her famous eve of Parliament receptions, she nevertheless found his effusive attentions mildly embarrassing. To begin with, he was not a Conservative, and a Labour leader besotted with a Conservative hostess was bound to lead to trouble, if only for him. MacDonald himself was aware of the pitfalls. 'Promise to let me judge', he wrote to her from Chequers in September, 1930, 'whether accepting invitations from you damages me or not. My fear is that you may be injured amongst your folks by asking me to sit at your table. And for harbouring these hesitations as to what people will say, are we not fools?'

Fools or not, they were locked in a mutually satisfying and powerful enough embrace for Lady Londonderry to continue with the friendship until Ramsay MacDonald's death, by which time her affection for him had strengthened until it resisted all attempts to undermine it. After his death, Chips Channon wrote, 'Few will regret him . . . Defiant at first, he soon took to grandeur and high life and wallowed in it like a man who has been

starving all his life. . . .' Lady Londonderry wrote more kindly of her old admirer:

He loved beautiful things – books, pictures, beautiful women. . .And why shouldn't he? He was, for these days, an old-fashioned Socialist. He fought against privilege and inequality of opportunity. . .When equality of opportunity – witness his own career – had been achieved, and he had time and leisure to review the past, I know he was dissatisfied and greatly disappointed with most of the leaders of his party. . . .

No wonder her rivals gnashed their teeth in frustrated envy. She had a talent for perceptive friendship that few could hope to equal.

Certainly Mrs Ronald Greville, for all her mythical wealth and her belief that she was able to influence international affairs, did not have Lady Londonderry's charm. She was the only daughter of John McEwen, a Scottish millionaire brewer, Liberal Member of Parliament and Privy Councillor, who, like Sir Ernest Cassel and others, made a number of profitable financial transactions for Edward VII. She filled her houses – 16 Charles Street and Polesden Lacey, near Dorking in Surrey – with financiers, ambassadors and foreign

Below: Ramsay MacDonald, the Labour prime minister, became a passionate admirer of Lady Londonderry despite their political differences.

royalty in the fond hope that by so doing she was 'preserving the peace of nations' (she once claimed that she had prevented Lord Lloyd from being made Viceroy of India). She had a consuming passion for royalty; English was best, of course, but anything, even deposed Balkan princes, was better than nothing. Like Lady Montdore in *Love in a Cold Climate* she 'loved them as much in exile as in power'. Just to say 'Sir' or 'Ma'am' and to sink into a curtsey, however clumsy, was manna to her soul.

Luckily for Mrs Greville, she did not have to depend too much on the Balkans. Queen Mary often went to tea at Polesden Lacey, usually at about six hours' notice – just enough time for Mrs Greville to get out her red carpet (like Mrs Grace Vanderbilt she was fond of saying 'One gets through so many red carpets in a season') – and the Duke and Duchess of York went there for their honeymoon. Queen Mary was doubtless attracted by the plethora of collectable objects littered all over the house. Mrs Greville must have been the ideal hostess for the Queen, whose notorious habit of admiring a valuable picture or antique in such a way as to oblige it to be pressed upon her as a gift made her an unwelcome visitor to those less besotted by her royal status.

The actual size of her fortune gave rise to much speculation. Mrs Greville herself maintained a sphinx-like detachment, only remarking occasionally that she was going to leave all her money to the rich. In the end,

when her will was finally published in 1942, she was found to have a mere £1,750,000 – presumably the result of a lifetime's dedication to the affairs of the rich and titled. She carried her infatuation with royalty to the grave. She left all her jewellery, including a sapphire and diamond ring said to have belonged to Catherine the Great, to the Queen, £20,000 to Princess Margaret and £25,000 to the Queen of Spain, whose daughter's dentist's bills, she once boasted to Harold Nicholson, she had paid.

Her epitaphs were not flattering. Harold Nicholson described her as 'nothing more than a fat slug filled with venom' and Cecil Beaton called her 'a galumphing, greedy, snobbish old toad who watered at her chops at the sight of royalty and the Prince of Wales's set and did nothing for anybody except the rich.'

Emerald Cunard, on the other hand, he remembered more kindly. 'For all her fantasies and foibles', he wrote after her death in 1948, 'she was a woman who lived *dans le vrai*. Someone as rough and rowdy as Lady Astor could never appreciate Emerald's subtlety, and quite wrongly judged her "a pushin'" American.' It would, indeed, be quite wrong to think of Lady Cunard as an adventuress, even though she had been born Maud Burke in San Francisco of French and Irish parents and had, as Kenneth Clark put

Above: A house party gathering at Sutton Place, the home of the Duke and Duchess of Sutherland. The guests included the King of Iraq, Mrs Greville and the Duchess of Northumberland.

Below left: Lady Cunard at the Strauss Ball with the Maharajah of Alwar.

Below: The Hon Mrs Greville (*left*) at Cannes for the winter season.

Above: A portrait of Cecil Beaton, the fashionable society photographer.

Right: Sir Bache Cunard, who provided Lady Cunard with the money which enabled her to secure a position for herself in Society.

it, 'wandered about Europe with her mother in search of adventures', and even though, as she put it herself, she moved in a 'whirlwind of passionate love affairs'.

Her first passionate attachment was to George Moore, whom she considered to be a writer as overpowering as Emile Zola. They met in 1894, when she was invited to a lunch party at the Savoy Hotel, saw he was a fellow guest and switched their name cards so that she could sit next to him. Most fortuitously he brought up the subject of Zola, holding forth at some length on what the French writer had achieved for the cause of freedom of expression in France. Maud, intoxicated, laid her 'fernlike' hand on his arm and declared, 'George Moore, you have a soul of fire.' He was equally captivated. 'Her courage, independence, her intellectual audacity . . . captured my admiration . . . I admired her cold sensuality, cold because it was divorced from tenderness and passion. I loved but an immortal goddess descended once more among men.'

Unfortunately for George Moore, Maud's mother decided that he was not only too old (he was forty eight) but not at all eligible enough for her talented daughter, and she whisked her back to America. There, after an unsatisfactory encounter with a Polish prince, Maud met Sir Bache Cunard, a grandson of the founder of the shipping line, and although he was forty three, he had the advantage of being very rich. So, with her mother's consent, they were married and soon afterwards they moved to Sir Bache's country house, Nevill Holt, which was situated in prime hunting country, near Market Harborough.

'Country life', wrote her biographer, Daphne Fielding, 'was a new experience for Maud, but she did not enjoy the novelty.' It was all very well cutting a dash while hunting, but what of the long hours in between? To begin with she occupied herself by re-arranging the furniture, 'banishing all the Victorian impedimenta and replacing them with solid, simple pieces in oak', reading Balzac and Shakespeare and giving birth to her daughter, Nancy. Then she cast around for livelier company with which to spend Saturday to Monday than her husband's sporting friends.

Since her marriage she had continued to correspond with George Moore, and he soon became a frequent visitor. The Prince of Wales took a liking to her and by so doing converted many of the stuffier members of society who had been wondering if this little yellow-haired American was good enough for them. It became fashionable to visit Nevill Holt – the Duchess of Rutland, Lady Randolph Churchill, Max Beerbohm, Somerset Maugham and Henry James were all prepared

to make the journey to Market Harborough regularly, lured as much by the unpredictability of their hostess as by the luxury and the excellence of the food.

In 1911, at a dinner in London, Maud met Sir Thomas Beecham and, true to her whirlwind nature, fell in love with him at first sight. Sir Bache was abandoned and she took a house in Cavendish Square, which she rented from the Prime Minister, Herbert Asquith, so that she would be able to devote herself and her considerable private fortune to helping Sir Thomas in his task of injecting new energy into English musical life.

In this house, and in the others she was to occupy, at Carlton House Gardens and No 4 Grosvenor Square, she created a unique setting for her parties, redolent of the newly arrived Ballet Russe, and a far cry from the Tudor style of Nevill Holt. Arsenic-green lamé curtains hung at the dining room windows and against one, according to Daphne Fielding, stood 'a black lacquer screen of carved porcupines framed in the nimbus of their bronze quills', and on another hung a

Left: Lady Cunard fell in love at first sight with Sir Thomas Beecham and left her husband, Sir Bache Cunard, to live with Beecham in Cavendish Square.

Right: A portrait of Lady Diana Cooper by Cecil Beaton. Lady Cunard introduced Lady Diana to guests as 'the most beautiful woman in the world'.

Below: Sybil Colefax, an avid collector of celebrities, seen with Rex Whistler, one of her 'young people'.

drop-cloth painted by the American artist Robert Winthrop Chanler, 'representing a forest of gentle leaf-eating giraffes, with light and shade pranking the trunks of the silvery birch trees.' In the middle of the room was the dining room table 'a huge circle of lapis lazuli, in the centre of which, reflecting the candle-light, stood a gilt-bronze epergne supported by naked figures of nymphs and naiads.'

Those lucky enough to get an invitation were in for a theatrical treat. To begin with there was the anticipation. 'One was invited for 1.30 p.m.', wrote Alan Jenkins, 'and had to wait, stomach rumbling with hunger until two o'clock, when Emerald made her entrance: as she did so, a servant switched on the central chandelier of the white and gold drawing room.' Then 'in her husky little voice, like a corncrake, she would make some absurd and shrill comment on her own arrival. "My maid is furious with me – she says . . . she

Left: Ivor Novello, popular composer and actor, first appeared on the regular stage in London in 1921. He was a prize no hostess could resist.

hasn't had time to straighten my eye-lashes . . .'" After that came the introductions. 'This is Lady Diana Cooper, the most beautiful woman in the world. This is Winston Churchill, the greatest orator since John Bright. This is Mr Michael Arlen the only Armenian who hasn't been massacred. . . .' The hypnotized guests then settled down to bounce the conversational ball, an art at which their hostess excelled.

It was, as Kenneth Clark said, an undiluted diet of hors d'oeuvres. One was allowed to be banal or inconsequential, but woe betide the pedant that reared his ugly head and to be too profound or to talk for too long was unforgiveable. 'I sometimes talked for about a minute on end, to the fury of the other guests; but Emerald forgave me.'

Others were not let off so lightly. On one occasion a rich American called Myron Taylor was subjected to a characteristically provocative opening question. 'Now, Mr Taylor, what do you think about incest?' 'Well, er . . . there seems to be no doubt at all that biologically the results are deleterious. In some of our small prairie towns statistics show . . .' 'But, Mr Taylor, what about Siegmund and Sieglinde.' And so on; the unhappy Mr Taylor, 'sweating profusely', retired in confusion, covering 'his large senatorial face with a table napkin', while Lady Cunard illustrated her point by singing in her small, sweet voice appropriate bits from the end of Act I of the *Valkyrie*.

On 2 April 1936 Harold Nicholson went to a dinner given by Mrs Simpson 'to meet the King'. His fellow guests included Lady Oxford, Lady Cunard and Lady Colefax. Both Mrs Simpson and the King were in high spirits, Mrs Simpson seeming blissfully unaware of the undercurrents of hostility circulating among the three ladies, each of whom was outraged that the other had been invited. As Harold Nicholson recorded in his diary: 'It is evident that Lady Cunard is incensed by the presence of Lady Colefax, and that Lady Colefax is furious that Lady Cunard should also have been asked. Lady Oxford appears astonished to find either of them at what was to have been a quite intimate party. . .'

No-one else would have had the confidence to commit such a gaffe, for it was well known that there was little love lost between hostesses competing in the same field. Lady Oxford once remarked crossly that she was not fond of Sybil Colefax, 'I don't care who people know, and it is so tiresome that Sybil is always on the spot. One can't talk about the birth of Christ without that Astrakhan ass [a slighting reference to Lady Colefax's mop of curly dark hair] saying she was there in the manger.'

This observation was not as unjust as it might seem. Lady Colefax's need to collect celebrities verged on the addictive (Osbert Sitwell referred to her house in the King's Road as 'Lion's Corner House'). Once she had marked down her prey she stalked it with all the predatory cunning of the obsessive lapidopterist, and once netted, she put her captives in a private glass case to be catalogued strictly in order of rarity value.

Then, her new specimens safely under lock and key, she wrote dozens of letters of invitation to lunch and dinner. The recipients would either be urged to 'come and meet my young people' or proffered another, more obviously attractive bait, such as H G Wells or Max Beerbohm. They rarely refused – possibly knowing that if they did they would be unlikely to get a second chance, but more often than not because, as Kenneth Clark said, 'it would have been a mistake to do so. Sybil was an excellent hostess. Her house was

Right: Somerset Maugham, talented novelist and a British agent during both World Wars, as portrayed by P Steegman in 1931. His wife Syrie left him when he left with his secretary, Gerald Haxton.

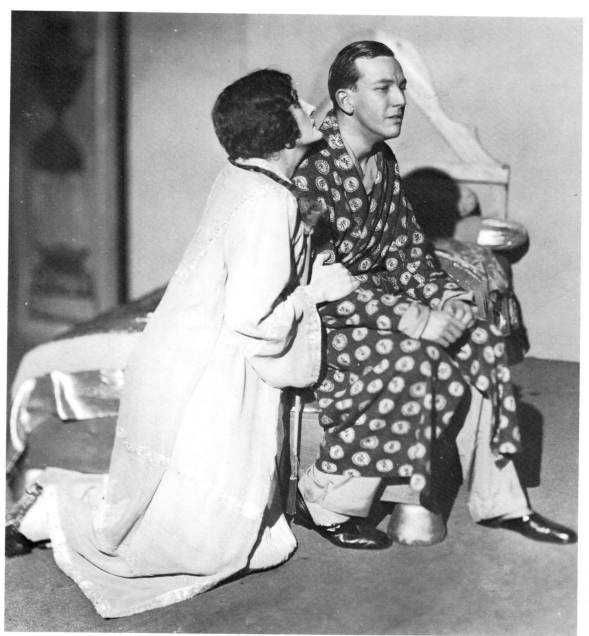

Left: Noel Coward and Lilian Braithwaite in one of Coward's first successful plays, *The Vortex*, at The Everyman Theatre in 1924. His plays were renowned for their biting humour and witty dialogue.

Below: One of Lady Colefax's interior designs. She started a vogue for striped chintz, and the income from her profitable business enabled her to entertain in a lavish manner.

pretty, and the company nearly always amusing. She was a well-read woman, who could stimulate the conversation of her literary guests. One met people one would never have met otherwise.'

One of her choicest specimens was Noel Coward, whom she captured long before anyone else had noticed him, tracking him down to the Everyman Theatre in Hampstead, where he was appearing in *The Vortex*. Other 'young people' included John Gielgud, Ivor Novello, Harold Nicholson, Cecil Beaton, Rex Whistler, Beverley Nichols, the Oliviers and the Kenneth Clarks.

The culmination of all her ambitions came when she was able to add the Prince of Wales and Mrs Simpson to her list. It was, therefore, particularly galling for Lady Colefax to find Lady Cunard and Lady Oxford at the 'little gathering to meet the King'. Under her horrified gaze her star exhibits seemed to be

Above: A Beaton portrait of Rex Whistler, a fine painter who also ventured into theatre design.

Top far right: Syrie Maugham, a society hostess who rivalled Mrs Colefax as hostess and interior designer. Her most popular look was the all-white room.

Below and bottom right: Two rooms in Syrie Maugham's flat. The all-white look went out of fashion when people realized it quickly became grubby.

slipping from her grasp, and it was no wonder her indignation knew no bounds.

A few months later, however, she re-established her primacy by persuading the King and Mrs Simpson to dine with her at Argyll House. The party on 11 June 1936 was both the climax of her career and her swan-song as a hostess. Her husband, Sir Arthur Colefax, an eminent King's Council but a man of few words at dinner parties (so few, indeed, that he was considered by many to be the biggest bore in England) had died in February. Lady Colefax, although she came from a prosperous middle-class background – Walter Bagheot and the Wedgewoods were among her ancestors – felt that she could no longer manage to keep up the house without the income that he had provided.

The evening was not an unqualified success. After dinner Arthur Rubinstein opened up the piano, announcing that he was going to play the 'Barcarolle'. When it became obvious to the King that this was not, as he had anticipated, the 'Barcarolle' from the *Tales of Hoffman*, he began to fidget, and, when he could bear it no longer, said, 'That isn't the one we like.' Rubinstein, undaunted, launched into more Chopin – a prelude. Then, as Kenneth Clark recorded, the King 'looked even more irritated, and at the end rose to leave. It was 10.15. Consternation. Sybil on the verge of tears. Lady Diana Duff Cooper took command, and asked Noel Coward to play one of his songs. . . .' Soon the strains of 'Mad Dogs and Englishmen' could be heard. The King went back into the drawing room and stayed for another hour and the party was saved.

One of Lady Colefax's more profitable sidelines was interior decoration. In this and in other ways she was in direct competition with her next door neighbour, Syrie Maugham. Mrs Maugham, who left her husband after his departure with his secretary, Gerald Haxton, was not only a lady of considerable social acumen but also a decorator of original and innovative talent. Although she did not share Lady Colefax's insatiable appetite for celebrities she was, nevertheless, eager to surround herself with the more gifted and personable members of society and, having obtained a handsome divorce settlement from her first husband, Henry Wellcome, and with the advantage of an unlimited charge account at Selfridges from her lover, Gordon Selfridge, was in a position to do so.

While she was married to Maugham she started a small decorating and antique shop in Baker Street and, deaf to his furious remarks about 'being in trade' and doing nothing but 'sell chamberpots to millionairesses', made so much money that she was able to move to Duke Street, on the corner of Grosvenor Square.

By the time she left him in 1927 her most successful decorative venture – the all-white look – was in full swing. It was a bug that bit fashionable living-rooms on both sides of the Atlantic with the virulence of an epidemic. Everyone everywhere who could afford it copied Mrs Maugham's Chelsea drawing room, where, as Cecil Beaton wrote, she had 'bleached, pickled or scraped every piece of furniture in sight. White sheepskin rugs were strewn on the eggshell surfaced floors, vast white sofas were flanked with crackled white incidental tables, white ostrich and peacock feathers were put in white vases against white walls. . . .' Even the flowers were white – arum lilies, white gardenias, white camellias and iceberg roses – and whole effect was one of 'a strange and marvellous surprise'.

There were a few dissenting voices. Lady Oxford advised her against so much hygenic whiteness: 'Dear Mrs Maugham, what you really need are a few old varnished maps on the walls . . .' and her estranged husband (who never had a good word to say for her) accused her of stealing the idea from an acquaintance, the wife of a Sandgate coal merchant, whose all-white drawing room Syrie had visited shortly before embarking upon the project herself.

From the other side of the fence Lady Colefax could only gnash her teeth in impotent fury. Later she got her revenge when, in partnership with John Fowler, she started a vogue for Regency-style striped chintz and Madame Recamier *chaise longues*. She introduced them at just about the time the rage for white ended – when, as Somerset Maugham had predicted, 'people discovered it became grubby and had to be redecorated'. And, of course, she had all her young people, while Syrie was often reduced to shameless bouts of spying. As Beverley Nichols wrote in his memoirs, he was once asked to, 'stand on a wheelbarrow and look over the garden wall to see whether Sybil Colefax had succeeded in luring Charlie Chaplin to lunch or not. . . .' The lionesses were in full cry and the hunt was up. It was everyone for herself.

A lioness with no pretensions to subtlety

Above: Gordon Selfridge, an American industrialist who started the highly successful store in London. He became Syrie Maugham's lover, and gave her an unlimited charge account at his store.

persuade the *crème de la crème* of Cleveland society to come to her parties met with a disappointing response. She moved to New York, which was even worse, and in 1922, as a last resort, she cashed all her steel shares and sailed for London.

This manoeuvre was more successful. Few people could resist the ingenious snares laid by the curious new arrival from Cleveland. To begin with she rented Mrs George Keppel's house in Grosvenor Street, on condition that Mrs Keppel's guest list should be included in the lease. At first the long list of dukes and duchesses huffily declined her invitations – after all, who was she? Nothing but a jumped-up little American with a painted face, who was said to have gone bald in early life and taken to wearing wig.

Mrs Corrigan, however, was not going to be defeated. She hired a social secretary, who had once worked for Lady Londonderry, and sent out some more invitations, this time offering a discreet bribe in the form of a cabaret from Paris and tombola. The prizes turned out to be gold cigarette cases, gold sock suspenders, gold vanity cases and tortoise-shell combs inlaid with gold, all from Cartier, and other trinkets of lesser value, such as silver pencils. Oddly enough, the winners of the most valuable objects turned out to be the dukes and duchesses and those of the more modest prizes the rest of the aristocratic guests, in strict order of precedence. 'After some years', wrote Loelia, Duchess of Westminster, 'it dawned on us that never by any chance were the prizewinners commoners, in fact they always happened to be the highest ranking people present.'

The lesser aristocracy might jib at discovering that the tombola was always rigged in favour of their peers but they succumbed completely to the fascination of seeing what the extraordinary Laura Corrigan would get up to next.

She rarely disappointed them. She had a habit of giving instructions to her butler 'that anyone who came to the door was to be given a cocktail – the butcher's boy, the Duke of York, the dressmaker, other people's chauffeurs.' She had a fascinating collection of wigs, 'a perfectly set one. . .a windswept one, a very dishevelled one . . .' and was famed for her malapropisms: 'my little *ventre a terre*' (of her Grosvenor Street House), 'the flying buttocks were magnificent' (of a cathedral), 'I did have a letter of introduction to them but I haven't sent it' (after a cruise, when asked if she had seen the Dardanelles).

There was no end to the fun society had with her. They gossiped behind her back, and told each other of the time Prince George came to dinner and instead of curtseying she welcomed him by standing on her head: or

was Laura Corrigan. The daughter of a Wisconsin carpenter, she conceived an undying passion for the rich and famous at an early age. She first married a house physician at the Chicago hotel where she was working as a waitress but her second marriage, soon afterwards, brought her within reach of her goal. James Corrigan was very rich – he owned a steel company – and he proved it at once by giving his new bride a $17,000 Rolls Royce complete with chauffeur and footman as a wedding present. Unfortunately for Laura, she soon became aware that her husband, for all his money, did not mix with the right people. Real Society, the old-fashioned died-in-the-wool sort, was closed to them. It appeared to be an insoluble problem. However, James Corrigan was a man of extreme sensibility and was prepared to do anything to make his wife happy. Quite soon, therefore, he did the best possible thing and died, leaving her an income of $800,000 a year.

Despite the munificence with which she splashed her money about, her attempts to

Left and below: Mr Fowler's showroom *(left)* and one of his interior designs *(below)*. He went into business with Lady Colefax and helped create the vogue for Regency-style striped chintz.

Right and below right: Two
Roger Fowler interiors from
the 1930s.

Below: Laura Corrigan, an
American who managed to
find a niche in the charmed
circle of English society, and
maintained it partly by her
intriguingly eccentric
behaviour.

the time she dived into Lord Dudley's swimming pool at Henley and her toupee, with its bathing cap firmly stuck to it, came off and she stayed under water until she had replaced it. They asked each other if they had heard that Lady Cunard, when asked by Mrs Corrigan if she was going to wear a tiara for a gala night at Covent Garden, replied, 'No, dear, just a small emerald bandeau and my own hair'; or if they had been at the party where she had danced the Charleston in a top hat and red-heeled shoes and at the end stood on her head, a scarf tied round her skirt 'for the sake of modesty'. Such strange behaviour endeared her to London Society.

At long last Mrs Corrigan had achieved her life's ambition. No amount of mocking could conceal the fact that everyone wanted to go to her parties. In 1940 the *Daily Mail* recorded that 'millionairess Laura Corrigan, one of the leading London hostesses over the past two decades, had moved into the Ritz Hotel in Paris, where her first-floor suite was said to run the entire length of the building.' She, at least, had no inhibitions about being called a hostess. It was all she had ever wanted to be.

Left: Mrs Corrigan at a garden party in Hanover Lodge. She enlivened British Society with her malapropisms.

Artists and Intellectuals

'We have just got to know a wonderful Lady Ottoline Morrell', wrote Virginia Stephen in 1909, 'who had the head of a Medusa; but she is very simple and innocent in spite of it, and worships the arts.' Lady Ottoline had just paid a visit to one of Virginia and her brother Adrian's Thursday evenings at their house in Fitzroy Square. She brought with her Dorelia and Augustus John.

They must have been an extravagant-looking trio. Lady Ottoline was tall and majestic and wore long, highly coloured dresses, strung about with pearls and amethysts; she wore her dark-red hair looped up on top of her head and her prominent nose jutted from her pale, thickly powdered face. Dorelia, equally tall, favoured outlandish gipsy clothes, a riot of reds and greens; Augustus, in a black frock coat and wide-brimmed hat, provided a foil for the parrot brilliance of the women's unusual apparel.

The impact that they made on the serious-minded members of the Stephen household was considerable. It was not just their picturesque appearance; it was the whiff of blatant heterosexuality that surrounded them – very different from the atmosphere of restrained celibacy, tempered by brief excursions into limp homosexual liaisons, as unthreatening as they were passionless, that prevailed inside 29 Fitzroy Square. The sight of three such richly plumaged birds of prey stalking in their midst put the languid, passive Bloomsbury group, with its vaguely platonic ideals and tepid infatuations, into a dither of heightened expectation.

So, later, when Lady Ottoline wrote to Virginia asking for the names and addresses of all her 'wonderful' friends they were instantly supplied. She had captured them all – Lytton Strachey, Saxon Sydney Turner, Clive and Vanessa Bell, Desmond McCarthy, Maynard Keynes, and Virginia herself – and lured them into her net. They went without protest, for as Virginia wrote:

'we were all swept into that extraordinary whirlpool where such odd sticks and straws were brought momentarily together. There was Augustus John very sinister (?) in a black stock and a velvet coat, Winston Churchill very rubicund all gold lace and medals on his way to Buckingham Palace; Raymond Asquith crackling with epigrams. . . . There was Lord Henry Bentinck at one end of the sofa and perhaps Nina Lamb at the other. There was Philip [Morrell] fresh from the House of Commons humming and hawing on the hearthrug. There was Gilbert Cannan who was said to be in love with Ottoline. There was Bertie Russell, whom she was said to be in love with. Above all, there was Ottoline herself.'

There was no doubt that much of the attraction of visits to the Morrell house in Bedford Square and, after the First World War, to

Previous page: (left to right), Rex Whistler, Cecil Beaton, Georgia Sitwell, William Walton, Stephen Tennant, Zita Jungman and Tessa Jungman in fancy dress costume, Cambridge 1923.

Above: Lady Ottoline in a characteristically flamboyant hat.

Above left: Lady Ottoline on the beach in Venice.

Left: The Green Room at Garsington Manor. Ottoline had a fine collection of paintings and books.

Right: The beauty of Garsington Manor itself was a draw to writers, poets and intellectuals.

Garsington Manor, near Oxford, lay in the sensational nature of Lady Ottoline herself. Born in 1872, she was the daughter of General Arthur Cavendish Bentinck and was a half-sister to the Duke of Portland. When her brother succeeded to the title, she and her mother, Lady Bolsover, moved into Welbeck, the Portland family seat. She was not, however, destined to become a conventional Victorian débutante. Strongly imaginative and romantic by temperament and with an unquenchable desire to liberate her senses through poetry, art and music, she looked about for more sympathetic ways in which to satisfy her craving for spiritual rapture.

At first she immersed herself in the evangelical movement, holding bible-classes for her mother's footmen, but soon (much to the relief of the footmen, who found these gatherings acutely embarrassing) abandoned them in favour of foreign travel. For months on end she roamed around Europe, especially in Italy, accompanied by a friend and a governess, soaking up the beauties of art and nature. Eventually she came home and settled down to consolidate her new-found knowledge through courses of serious study at St

Andrews and Oxford. While she was at Oxford she met Philip Morrell and although she had her doubts: 'I didn't really think of marrying . . . and clung to my solitary liberty . . . I believe in many women there is a strong intuitive feeling of pride in their solitary life that when marriage really comes it is, to a certain extent, a humiliation . . .' they were married at St Peter's, Eaton Square, on 8 February 1902.

Far from being a humiliation, marriage for Lady Otteline was the stepping-stone on which she could cross from the amorphous world of youthful self-discovery to the harmonious existence 'lived on the same plane as poetry and music' she had yearned for all her life. In Philip Morrell she had found the ideal partner in such an enterprise for, after a brief career as a Liberal member of Parliament, followed by an excursion into pacifism, he retreated to Garsington Manor and led the unobtrusive life of a cultivated gentleman farmer, leaving his wife free to surround herself with as many artists, writers and intellectuals as she could persuade to visit her at Garsington.

They came willingly enough. Her striking

Below left: Lytton Strachey *(left),* the biographer who challenged Victorian self-assurance, painter Duncan Grant *(centre),* and art and literary critic Clive Bell were just a few of the artistic and literary lions of the day who met at Ottoline's home.

Below: Phillip Morrell married Ottoline in 1902. He led a quiet and cultivated existence, leaving Ottoline free to entertain.

Left: Augustus John made an
early reputation for himself
with his etching. Lady
Ottoline conceived a violent
passion for him and pursued
him with fervour.

Above: Virginia Woolf, a member of the Bloomsbury Group which met in private houses in London in the 1920s for philosophic and artistic discussion. Her impressionistic style of writing is a development of the stream-of-consciousness technique.

Right: A painting of Bertrand Russell by Roger Fry. Russell's controversial writings on philosophy, morals and politics led to him being imprisoned in 1918 for his outspoken pacifism.

appearance, her inquisitiveness and her genuine passion for the life of the mind and spirit, together with the extreme beauty of her house and garden, made visits to Garsington as desirable to members of the intellectual élite as the villa outside Florence must have been to the group of young patricians who met there regularly during the plague in order to discuss history, painting and literature and to tell the stories of Boccaccio.

The house, too, as in Boccaccio, was full of sensuous delights and dramatic combinations; patricians, Celts, fox-hunting poets, wild artists, Oxford men, Cambridge men, orthodox Anglicans, atheists, scientists and philosophers were jumbled together in a riot of sympathetic disorder, confronted on all sides by tangible signs of their achievements, which festooned the walls and littered the tables. Paintings by Walter Sickert, Mark Gertler, Henry Lamb, Augustus John and Duncan Grant hung alongside Italian artists and *The Rainbow*, *Ulysses*, the *Outline of Philosophy* and the poems of Yeats lay among copies of Meredith, Thackeray and the *Leviathan*.

Whether her guests were sitting by the warmth of the incense-laden fires in the Venetian red drawing room or strolling among the ilex trees and Italian statues reflected in the lake, their hostess, as enticing as Madonna Dianora, moved among them in a trance of exquisite satisfaction, her deep voice throbbing with emotional zeal, as she drew from her favourites the succour she needed. Virginia Woolf wrote:

With what imperious directness, like that of an artist intolerant of the conventional and humdrum . . . [Ottoline] singled out the people she admired for qualities that she was often the first to detect and champion, and brought them together . . . Whether she sat at her table against a background of pale yellow and pomegranate, or mused. . .with her embroidery on her lap and undergraduates at her feet . . . she created her own world.

It was a world in which the possesssion of creative gifts was of paramount importance. Accidents of birth, religious belief or lack of it paled into insignificance beside concrete manifestations of talent. Lady Ottoline might find T S Eliot's dislike of Shelley and paganism distressing (as Stephen Spender remarked, 'Greece, Italy, Plato, Phidias, Michelangelo and Shelley were for her pure evocations of Truth, Goodness and Beauty), but when he defended Christianity she felt, with Lord David Cecil, that she had 'been given a glimpse into the depths of Eliot's grand and tragic spirit' and forgave him.

Although Lady Ottoline suffered two particularly tempestuous affairs of the heart – with Augustus John, whom she pursued with relentless fervour, showering him with expensive presents and peppering him with invitations to tragic melodramas and concerts of love music, and with Bertrand Russell – her main emotional preoccupation was with the lives of her *protégés*. Her inquisitiveness knew no bounds. As Stephen Spender put it, 'Thoroughly incapable of being shocked by anything human, she wished her friends to contribute their most intimately dramatic qualities to the *commedia* which was her home. "Does your friend have no Love-Life?" she complained once to a poet who had brought a somewhat reticent friend to tea.'

Understandably she came up against some resistance from those who wished to protect their emotional privacy, and when she did, as with Siegfried Sassoon, she was both baffled and hurt. She wrote:

I find Siegfried very sympathetic and attractive and my instinct goes out to him for he seems so intimate to me, as if he were a twin brother . . . I find it a great joy to be with any one so human and aware of ordinary life, after the intellectuals who walk along half-blind. Sometimes I feel that in him I have found that wonderful companion that I have so much desired, who would drink of the fountain of many colours that springs up in my inner self; but he is very aloof and obviously doesn't need my friendship. . . .

There were other disappointments. The publication of *Crome Yellow* in 1921 was a bitter blow, for although its reception confirmed Lady Ottoline's own opinion of the promise Aldous Huxley had shown as a Balliol undergraduate during the First World War, no amount of dazzling literary pyrotechnics could make up for the cynicism of the thinly disguised portrait of Garsington and its *habitués*, and no amount of placatory letters from Aldous could dispel the feeling of betrayal.

D H Lawrence, too, put his foot in it with *Women In Love*. Hermione Roddice, whose 'shoes and stockings were brownish grey, like the feathers on her hat, her hair was heavy , she drifted along with a peculiar fixity of the hips, a strange unwilling motion . . . [a] woman of the new school, full of intellectuality, and heavy, nerveworn with consciousness . . . [who was] passionately interested in reform, her soul . . . given up to the public cause' and who was, in essence, a man's woman, did not find favour in Lady Ottoline's eyes. She herself, surely, had more substance. What about her immense understanding and her feeling for beauty?

Both these defections caused open quarrels and subsequent rifts. She never forgave either of them their treachery, although in the end she patched things up superficially with the Huxleys. But an element of trust had vanished and in 1928 the Morrells left Garsington for ever. They moved to 10 Gower Street, where, on Thursday afternoons, they received their

Above: A portrait of Aldous Huxley by Cecil Beaton. *Crome Yellow*, Huxley's satire on post-war Britain, was a thinly disguised portrayal of Garsington Manor, and its publication led to a rift between Huxley and Lady Ottoline.

Left: Vanessa Bell, painted by Duncan Fry. A member of the Bloomsbury Group, she helped promote the works of Post-Impressionists through the Omega Workshops.

78

Above: Roger Fry held an exhibition of Post-Impressionists at Grafton Gallery in 1910, introducing the works of Van Gogh, Gauguin and Matisse to a British audience. The exhibition was hardly well received.

old friends, and their new ones, 'still chosen', as Lord David Cecil said, 'as likely to contribute to the life lived on the plane of poetry and of music, though the music was gentler and the poetry less impassioned than that which had echoed so resoundingly through the halls of Garsington during the hey-day of [their] life there.'

One relationship that never went sour (even though Virginia was capable of malicious remarks behind her back), was the friendship between the Morrells and Leonard and Virginia Woolf. In 1918 Virginia met Lady Ottoline again after an interval of several years and it was, as her nephew Quentin Bell wrote, 'a reunion which seems to have been highly gratifying to both ladies.' Virginia wrote to her sister, Vanessa Bell, 'I was so much overcome by her beauty that I really felt as if I'd suddenly got into the sea, and heard the mermaids fluting on their rocks . . . our conversation was rather on those lines, so I'm not surprised that I had made a good impression. . . .'

To inflame the imagination of Virginia Woolf was no mean feat – even though the letter ended on a less flattering note, observing that Ottoline was not so much 'of a fool as I'd been led to think; she was quite shrewd, though vapid in the intervals.' When Virginia's delicate mental health permitted, visits to Garsington followed the reunion.

This in itself was something of a triumph. The Woolfs were the focal point in a circle of their own – dominated by Virginia, her sister Vanessa and their brother Adrian Stephen – that had sprung from a group of Cambridge undergraduates in the late 1890s. The original members of this charmed circle, who were in many cases connected by blood or marriage, included another Stephen brother, Thoby, who died in 1906, Leonard Woolf, Lytton Strachey, Saxon Sydney Turner, Clive Bell, Maynard Keynes, Desmond McCarthy, Duncan Grant and, later, Roger Fry. Their aims were high-minded; nothing less than a complete clean sweep of prevailing orthodoxies was contemplated. As Clive Bell wrote, in an essay on his contemporaries, 'they shared a taste for discussion in the pursuit of truth and contempt for conventional ways of thinking and feeling, contempt for conventional morals, if you will.'

After they left Cambridge these elevated

views were mulled over incessantly at the Stephen's house in Bloomsbury but none of them managed to produce much evidence of the tremendous talents they felt burgeoning in their midst until 1910, when Roger Fry launched an exhibition of post-impressionist paintings at the Grafton Gallery. This exhibition had repercussions far in excess of its original aim, which was to introduce the British public to the works of Cézanne, Matisse and Picasso. It launched an aesthetic controversy that has raged ever since, between the champions of representational art and the exponents of non-representational art, and served as an exhilarating reminder to those committed to the Post Impressionist movement – in and out of Bloomsbury – that there must be no appeasement but war to the death.

The world, as Lytton Strachey pointed out in an essay entitled 'Avons nous changé tout cela?' had a long way to go before tolerance was a *sine qua non* – so far all that had been achieved was to effect a 'transition from the metaphysical to the ethical species of persecution. . . .' and 'after the late fulminations of Sir William Richmond, against Post-Impressionism, nobody could be very much surprised if a stake were set up tomorrow for Mr Roger Fry in the courtyard of Burlington House.'

The opprobrium that surrounded the exhibition was the Bloomsbury group's first taste

Left: The Illustrated London News' reaction to Roger Fry's Post-Impressionist exhibition. It noted that although many people visited the exhibition, few were favourably impressed.

of public execration and, in typically self-congratulatory style, they closed ranks and rallied the faithful into the fold. Vanessa Stephen, recently married to the critic Clive Bell, together with fellow artists such as Duncan Grant and Mark Gertler turned their attention to the Omega Workshops. These were founded in 1912 by Roger Fry in an attempt to further the cause of post-impressionism by helping young and penniless artists to find an outlet for their work through the decorative arts. From Vanessa's house at 33 Fitzroy Square they printed materials, decorated furniture and painted trays, fans, pots and bookplates in bold colours and abstract designs for the mass market.

If their products did not quite, as Roger Fry had hoped, 'sweep through the furniture shops of London', they did bear witness to the artistic members of the group's ability to transform their irreverent attitude to the die-hard art establishment into positive action. It was no longer time to be sceptical, it was time to be up and doing.

By 1920, the whole Bloomsbury group, born along on the crest of the artistic wave, was in full sail. Predominantly pacifist, most of its members remained untouched by the war, taking the view that the whole business was 'horrible, unnecessary and fundamentally ridiculous'. This flippant aproach earned them the dislike of many, notably H G Wells, who described them as 'genteel Whigs' and found their irreverence towards what he saw as essentially a matter of honour an affront to those who were daily risking their lives at the front. Undeterred by these taunts, Lytton Strachey settled down to write *Eminent Victorians*, which aptly drained the stuffing out of such hitherto inviolable idols as Florence Nightingale, Cardinal Manning, General Gordon and Thomas Arnold, and began *Queen Victoria.* Virginia Woolf wrote *The Voyage Out* and *Night and Day* and began *Jacob's Room.* Maynard Keynes produced *The Economic Consequences of the Peace* and Leonard Woolf together with his wife continued to print increasing numbers of their own works for their Hogarth Press, as well as that of Katherine Mansfield and T S Eliot, on the hand-press they had picked up for twenty pounds in the Farringdon Road.

Hard on the heels of these achievements came a softening of public opinion. Even Bloomsbury's harshest critics were forced to admit, by the mid-1920s, that now that the cost had been counted and the last horrors of war and famine had faded into the past, there might, after all, have been something to be said for a disbelief in war. Other taboos, too, had been laid to waste. Everyone now talked about sex and most people were able to see that Cézanne was not a madman or Picasso a charlatan. Bloomsbury, in short, became respectable. Virginia Woolf's linguistic juxta-positions, Lytton Strachey's acerbic wit, Roger Fry's avant-garde criticism, Maynard Keynes' revolutionary approach to economics, while exciting admiration, had ceased to shock. Gradually each member of the group

was absorbed into the very establishment from which they had taken such pains to separate themselves fifteen years before.

The Hogarth press made a profit, Maynard Keynes urged the Liberal party to make sexual liberty part of its official platform, Lytton Strachey became a grand old man of letters and Virginia Woolf moved into the *beau monde* and dined with Lady Colefax and Lady Cunard. Even her novel *Orlando*, published in 1928, which took as its principal theme the androgynous nature of men and women, was not so much an erotic fantasy as a hymn in praise of the aristocratic ideal, an ideal embodied by Vita Sackville-West, that exotic daughter of Knole, whose infatuation for her Virginia found irresistibly flattering.

In the wake of worldly success, the more subversive elements of Bloomsbury defected into other camps. Lytton Strachey, Clive Bell and Roger Fry, together with the young Cyril

Above: Edith and Osbert Sitwell. The Sitwells aimed to regenerate the arts and achieved a certain amount of notoriety, Osbert partly by the publication of *Before the Bombardment*. Edith wrote and presented *Façade* to a stormy reception, but it was Noel Coward's satire of her performance in *London Calling* which really hit the headlines.

Right: The Sitwell trio; Osbert *(left)*, Sacheverell *(centre)* and Edith *(right)*. Sacheverell was also a poet, though in a more traditional style than Edith. A respected art critic, he helped popularize the baroque.

Connolly (as androgynous as the best of them) veered between Gordon Square and 2 Carlyle Square, the London home of Osbert and Sacheverell Sitwell.

The fact was, it was a great deal more fun at the Sitwells. Instead of the austere atmosphere of Bloomsbury, there was a heady mixture of cultivated sensibility and aristocratic glamour. The combination of the two brothers' passion for strange and beautiful objects, their literary aspirations and their rich and effortless way of life was one that few aspiring bourgeois aesthetes wanted to miss. The house alone was a sight for starved aesthetic eyes as Alan Pryce Jones wrote:

There was a fine jumble, from sketches of decor for Diaghilev to the Neapolitan conch-shaped silver chairs round the dining-room table. Small pretty things abounded – the house was a temple of a now-forgotten style called "the amusing". And there would be music and delicious cocktails, very dry, preceded by a ritual in which the wet rims were dipped in icing sugar. It was most dashing.

On top of all this unaccustomed luxury, visitors to Carlyle Square were treated to the brothers themselves and, if she had been tempted from her separate lair in the Moscow Road, their elder sister, Edith. Together they presented a formidable trio. 'Believe me', wrote Loelia, Duchess of Westminster, 'it really was something to meet the Sitwells for the first time. . . . They were so utterly unlike anybody else, and held a position in the arts that no one aspires to today . . . They were so extraordinarily clever and funny and there were three of them. . . .'

All three had, in their own way, achieved considerable artistic notoriety, a fate by no means disagreeable to them. All had published poetry and Osbert and Sacheverell had launched themselves into the heady business of patronage. They began with music. In 1919, when he was still up at Oxford, Sacheverell came across William Walton, then seventeen and a music scholar at Christchurch, and, having heard him play part of a piano quartet he was writing, became convinced that he was a genius. To spare him the necessity of having to teach for a living, Sacheverell suggested that he and Osbert should adopt him and take him to live with them, so that his talents could be given full rein. It was, as the Sitwell's biographer, John Pearson, pointed out, 'a courageous decision. They had little money, they were neither of them musicians . . . (and they) were acting in the high-handed and expansive style of eighteenth-century patrons.' Apart from these considerations, there was some opposition from the musical establishment at Oxford, principally from Dr Strong, the Dean of

Above: William Walton at his piano. Patronized by the Sitwells, he wrote the music for *Façade*. His later compositions made more concessions to melody.

Christchurch and Dr Henry Lay, the college organist, who both thought their pupil would be better served by a course of study with Sir Charles Stanford at the Royal College of Music.

In the end Walton himself settled the matter and decided in favour of the Sitwells. He moved into Carlyle Square and for the next fourteen years shared his life with his eccentric benefactors – a decision he never regretted. 'If it hadn't been for them', he wrote, 'I'd either have ended up like Stanford, or would have been a clerk in some Midlands bank with an interest in music. Life would have been a very great deal duller.'

The next project was modern art. In 1919 Osbert visited Paris at the expense of Mrs Greville (who was worried about his health) and came back unable to contain his excitement at what he had found. Not only were the streets 'lined with galleries full of modern pictures' but also he had unearthed a painter called Modigliani, undoubtedly a great genius, but ill and starving, his unsavoury garret crammed with unsold pictures, and obviously in sore need of a patron.

The result of this flirtation with the modern movement was an exhibition of French art at the Mansard Gallery in the Tottenham Court Road, London, masterminded by Modigliani's melancholy Polish dealer, Zborowski, who knew a good thing when he saw it. Zborowski arranged not only for his *protégé's* work to come to London, but also for paintings by Derais, Vlaminck, Soutine, Matisse, Utrillo, Picasso and Dufy, in the hope that they would captivate British buyers. Unfortunately the time was not ripe – the British public reacted with uniform indifference. Drawings by Modigliani sold for a shilling each, and Osbert and Sacheverell bought *The Peasant Girl* for the paltry sum of four pounds. The rest of the stock returned to Paris unsold, after Osbert and Sacheverell had appealed unsuccessfully to their father, Sir George Sitwell, to buy them for a few hundred pounds as a job lot.

While all this activity was going on at 2 Carlyle Square, Edith was entertaining poets and writers to tea and buns in her lodgings in Pembridge Mansions in the Moscow Road. 'Those tea parties of hers really were one of the most extraordinary literary affairs of the twenties', wrote Geoffrey Gorer, 'when you think of them. For there she was, all but penniless, in a dingy little flat in an unfashionable part of London. All she could offer was

strong tea and buns. Yet because of who she was she attracted to that flat almost every major literary figure of the twenties. . . .' Apart from tea and sympathy, Edith had a more positive role to play. Unlike her two brothers, she was possessed of some musical sense, and, between 1920 and 1922 she had begun, as John Pearson said, 'her poetic "exercises"' – teaching herself to use words much as a composer uses notes and phrases in his music . . . she was experimenting to obtain through the medium of words the rhythm of dance measures such as waltzes, polkas, foxtrots.'

These experiments, naturally enough, intrigued William Walton, who was roped in to supply accompanying music – encouraged by Osbert and Sacheverell, who told him flatly that if he did not want to do it, they could always ask Constant Lambert to have a go.

Above: In the 1920s Cecil Beaton became famous for his Society photographic portraits, many of which appeared in *Vanity Fair* and *Vogue* magazines. He is seen here in his home.

Far left: Herself of aristocratic descent, Edith Sitwell rebelled against bourgeois philistinism.

Left: From the left, Ottoline Morrell, Maria Nys, Lytton Strachey, Duncan Grant and Vanessa Bell at one of Lady Ottoline's famous gatherings at Garsington Manor.

Above: 'The Swiss Family Whittlebot', Noel Coward's wicked satire of Edith Sitwell's *Façade*, was a hit with audiences at the Duke of York's Theatre in 1923.

With this unpalatable alternative at the back of his mind, Walton got down to business. After all, Schoenberg had written music to accompany Albert Giraud's *Pierrot Lunaire*, and there had been Cocteau's *Parade*, to music by Eric Satie. Why not *Façade*, with words by Edith Sitwell and music by William Walton?

In the end, it was not Schoenberg or Satie that influenced Walton, but Stravinsky's *The Soldier's Tale*, a complex score that included a waltz in the Viennese style, a ragtime serenade, an Argentinian tango and a Bach-like chorale. Edith borrowed Cocteau's idea of declaiming her verses through a megaphone, to give them added lustre. After much trial and error the final result was given a dress rehearsal in January 1922 before an audience of invited friends in the drawing room at Carlyle Square, as John Pearson described:

With varying degrees of bafflement and pleasure they heard what the typewritten programme officially described as "Miss Edith Sitwell on her Sengerphone with accompaniments, overture and interlude by W T Walton". The poems that she read included "Madame Mouse Trots", "Said King Pompey" and "Jumbo's Lullaby". Walton conducted his somewhat mutinous sextet behind the. . curtain . . . and the evening ended with placatory offerings of hot rum punch to all the audience.

Despite the dress rehearsal, the public performance, at the Aeolian Hall in Bond Street on 12 June 1923, did not go well. It was not quite the battle between an audience of Philistines and artists of unimpeachable integrity that the Sitwells claimed in their memoirs (a response that would have lent its own kind of distinction to the event). Rather, it produced a reaction of polite indifference. The audience, which included Harold Acton, Evelyn Waugh and Virginia Woolf, clapped dutifully and then drifted away into the summer night and forgot about it.

There were, however, some unexpected repercussions. In September 1923 *London Calling!*, a revue by Noel Coward, opened at the Duke of York's Theatre, the highspot of which was a sketch entitled 'The Swiss Family Whittlebot', in which Maisie Gay gave a spirited performance as the poetess Hernia Wittlebot reciting her poems with her two brothers, Gob and Sago. The allusion was unmistakeable and it was not one that even the publicity-hungry Osbert much cared for. As for Edith, she became ill with unhappiness. A stream of angry letters poured forth daily from Carlyle Square: 'Insulting my sister is a fine beginning for you', to which Coward replied cautiously and with a 'well-simulated air of puzzled apology', a response that deeply irritated Osbert and entirely failed to mollify his feelings of injured family pride.

The feud over *London Calling!* dragged on for years, but the sketch remained as popular as ever. The Whittlebots melted into folklore – there was even an anthology of Whittlebot poetry. Ironically, it was the publicity surrounding *London Calling!*, rather than *Façade*, that brought the Sitwells into the public eye and contributed to their transformation from three curious literary-minded aristocrats into cult figures. In reply to a letter asking 'Who are the Sitwells?' the editor of *The Star* responded, 'They are all poets. But they are more than that. They are a cult.'

It was the beginning of the great Sitwell legend. They became mythical beings possessed of almost magical powers. They had only to wave their wands and their protégés were turned into swans. A whole generation of Oxford-educated young men, with spiritual affinities to Cocteau and Diaghilev, and nurturing an unrequited passion for the 1890s, found in the Sitwells an embodiment of the myth of a romantic, artistic aristocracy. Brian Howard, Harold Acton, Evelyn Waugh, Peter Quennell, Cyril Connolly and Kenneth Clark were each in turn touched and influenced by their dress, manner and attitude to life.

Brian Howard affected clothes like Osbert's, Harold Acton recited Edith's poems through a megaphone from a college window and Evelyn Waugh vowed he would never again subject himself to the middle-class traumas of home life in Hampstead, but would henceforth live a life of shameless devotion to the aristocratic ideal; Cyril Connolly extolled their virtues as 'social and artistic paragons' and Kenneth Clark was delighted to 'find people so liberated from accepted thought and values – particularly from those of Bloomsbury and the domi-

nation of Roger Fry and all that muddy-coloured, pseudo-classicism.'

Perhaps the most devoted acolyte of all was Cecil Beaton. During his twenties, a time when he described himself as 'snobbish with artistic aspirations', he asked a worldly friend how he should conduct his life to his best advantage. His friend did not hesitate, 'I wouldn't bother too much being anything in particular. Just become a friend of the Sitwells and see what happens.' Beaton took his friend's advice and found the Sitwells' establishment quite intoxicating:

The Sitwell brothers. . .had established a mode of existence that completely satisfied my own taste. No detail of their way of life was ugly or humdrum. They managed to give a patina of glamour to a visit to an oculist, a bootshop, or a concert. Each catalogue they received from a wine merchant or a bookseller in their hands became a rare volume. With their aristocratic looks, dignified manner, and air of lofty disdain, they seemed to be above criticism. A whole new world of sensibility opened to me while sitting in candlelight around the marble dining table in Osbert's house in Chelsea.

No aspiring aesthete could ask for more.

Above and left: Cecil Beaton was one of the Sitwells most devoted admirers.

The Long
Extravaganza

'Really', wrote Noel Coward after re-reading his journals, 'my life has been one long extravaganza.' Apart from being accident-prone as a child, having to train with the Artists' Rifles for a few months in 1918 (an experience that made him physically ill), enduring the onset of a nervous breakdown in 1926 and the humiliation of being booed at the first night of *Sirocco*, he led a charmed life. From birth to death, his guardian angel hovered over him, making sure he had everything he needed.

First there was his looks; angelic as a child, romantic as a boy, debonair as a young man and impeccably suave for the rest of his life. Then there were his talents – he had his first professional engagement at the age of ten, at the Court Theatre in what was described as a 'Fairy Play in Three Acts with a Star Cast of Wonder Children' and from then on, except for a gap in 1914, he was never out of work. He was charming, when he was seventeen he had a modest part as an extra in the film *Hearts of the World* but far from languishing unseen he managed to make friends with the

two stars, Lillian and Dorothy Gish, and, more important still, with their mother, who invited him to share the lunch she brought to the studios every day. Then, above all, there was the manner of his death – at night, from a heart attack, having just put down a book by his favourite author, E Nesbit. 'To the last detail', as his biographer, Cole Lesley, wrote, 'Noel's life had been rounded off to perfection.'

The distribution of favours on earth has always been a subject for speculation and some suspicion. Fairy godmothers never leave the pages of fairy stories and are not considered serious subjects for allegorical myth. The legend of Faust has been given more serious attention – possibly because it is the antithesis of the Sermon on the Mount. The idea of storing up treasures on earth in the sure knowledge that retribution will come after death appeals to all human beings of little faith and tends to corrupt the half-hearted. It is difficult to believe, however, that Noel Coward succumbed to satanic temptation and entered into a pact with Mephistopheles for the rewards he reaped in his lifetime. For all his charm and apparent facility, he was made of sterner stuff. He had not Faust's soft underbelly of academic pretension, ever-vulnerable to flattery and cajolery, or his fatally self-destructive romantic streak. Coward's observations were always tempered by an irony well-equipped to match that of any adversary, malevolent or benign, and his wit was rooted in an affectionate realization of human fallibility.

The nearest he ever got to selling his soul was in the summer of 1924, when Sir James Dunn, a rich financier who had never taken the slightest notice of him before, suddenly announced that he was a genius and that he was prepared to give him one hundred pounds a month in return for twenty percent of his earnings over the next five years. With

Previous page: Noel Coward and Gertrude Lawrence in *Private Lives* in 1930. Coward wrote this play for Lawrence.

Right: Noel Coward as a baby.

Below: Coward's theatrical career began early. Here he takes the part of a mushroom in a ballet in 1912.

Far right: The successful playwright at work in 1935.

Above: Noel Coward dictates a musical composition to his secretary in 1925.

mixed reviews for *London Calling* and three plays, *The Vortex*, *Fallen Angels* and *Hay Fever*, gathering dust on the shelves of every management in the West End, it was a tempting proposition and Coward had to summon up all his courage to refuse.

This act of self-denial did not go unrecognized by his ethereal protectors. A few weeks later *The Vortex* was accepted by Norman MacDermott, manager of the Everyman Theatre, Hampstead, and after various ups and 'downs, which included the leading lady walking out a week before production, and a dress rehearsal so bad that not even the most theatrically superstitious among the cast believed it would be alright on the night, it opened in November 1924. It was an evening that has passed into the annals of theatre mythology, with the drama by no means confined to the stage. Hampstead was unfamiliar ground for West End audiences to tread, and the Everyman Theatre was very far from being The Haymarket. Nevertheless, driven

Right: Noel Coward and Lilian Braithwaite in *The Vortex*, his first hit. It drew Society audiences into the unknown territory of Hampstead, North London.

by some extrasensory power, fashionable London, dressed as usual in white tie and tails, furs and jewels, slithered along icy roads up the hill to the minute theatre and sat expectantly on the cramped wooden seats and waited to be entertained.

They were not disapointed. 'The audience', wrote Cole Lesley, 'was agreeably shocked by the first-act comedy dialogue and then genuinely startled by the abrupt switch to near-tragedy in the third, and by the highly-charged emotional tension of the acting.' Curtain call followed curtain call and Lilian Braithwaite, playing the well-preserved mother, and Noel Coward her drug-addicted son, found themselves besieged by an army of ecstatic admirers, pressing into their small dressing rooms or waiting outside the stage door to congratulate them. It was Noel Coward, as director and author as well as leading actor, who took the lion's share of the praise. Two weeks before his twenty-fifth birthday he became a star. He also became the prize no hostess worth her salt could fail to dangle before the jaded palates of her luncheon guests, and the incarnation of the bitter-sweet myth of the 1920s.

All over London young men were buying red satin dressing gowns and young women were struggling with ivory cigarette holders. In every restaurant cynical world-weary men with clean-cut profiles exchanged light-hearted badinage with gay, thin, provocative and self-assertive companions. Reality merged into theatricality and a sense of drama hovered over the lighting of a cigarette, the putting on of powder and lipstick, or the throwing of a fox fur around the shoulders.

At the centre of this drama of everyday life

"IT'S ENGLAND!"
The Evening News

" GRAND, STIRRING ENTERTAINMENT."
The Sunday Dispatch

" INSPIRING, BREATHTAKING "
News of the World

" A NATIONAL INFLUENCE "
The Sunday Express

" ITS PATRIOTISM IS ETERNAL "
Lancashire Daily Post

" A MAGNIFICENT PLAY "
The Daily Mail

" HELD ME SPELLBOUND "
The Daily Herald

" SOMETHING REALLY VITAL "
Yorkshire Telegraph

" THE TONIC THAT ENGLISHMEN NEED "
The Morning Post

" MOST BEAUTIFUL, STIMULATING, PATRIOTIC PLAY "
Glasgow Evening Times

" BREATHES INSPIRATION "
Western Evening Herald

" ' I hope,' said Mr. Coward, ' that this play has made us feel that despite our national troubles, it is still a pretty exciting thing to be English.' THAT, IN A NUT SHELL, IS ' CAVALCADE ' "
James Agate in The Sunday Times

" Charles B. Cochran and Noel Coward not only have staged a magnificent spectacular drama, but have gone far to re-waken that love of country of which England stands in such bitter need "
The Sporting Life

"Everybody is talking about it. Everybody should see it!"
The Evening Standard

Above: The chorus line from the revue *Words and Music* which played at the Adelphi Theatre in 1932.

Above left: Some of the reviews for *Cavalcade*, for which Coward also wrote the music.

Left: A composite photograph of Evelyn Laye as the young girl and the old lady in Coward's operetta *Bitter Sweet.*

Right: Gertrude Lawrence and Coward in *Private Lives* in 1930. This play explored the themes of divorce and adultery, previously taboo subjects.

was Noel Coward himself. Other dramatists might be successful and other actors write plays and songs, or become actor-managers, but no-one since Oscar Wilde could crackle with so many contemporary epigrams. No-one else could perform so many emotional sleights of hand, veering shamelessly from the cynical to the sentimental, or veil his sly digs at human fallibility with such effortless ease and charm. Others could only look and wonder and try not to use too many superlatives when writing about him. In 1927, after seeing *This Year of Grace*, St John Ervine wrote rapturously that it was 'the most amusing, the most brilliant, the cleverest . . . the most - uberous, the most versatile, the wittiest . . .' revue he had ever seen. On a more sober note, Virginia Woolf told him that 'some of the numbers struck me on the head like a bullet. And what's more I remember them and see them enveloped in atmosphere – works of art, in short.' In 1934, after he had completed *Bitter Sweet*, *Private Lives*, *Cavalcade* and *Words and Music*, Somerset Maugham wrote:

For us English dramatists the young generation has assumed the brisk but determined form of Mr Noel Coward. He knocked at the door with impatient knuckles, and then he rattled the handle, and then he burst in. After a moment's stupor the older playwrights welcomed him affably enough and retired with what dignity they could muster to the shelf which with a spritely gesture he indicated to them as their proper place . . . and since there is no-one now writing who has more obviously a gift for the theatre than Mr Noel Coward, nor more influence with young writers, it is probably his inclination and practice that will be responsible for the manner in which plays will be written during the next thirty years.

Not all elderly playwrights retired gracefully to their dusty shelves. Barrie, Shaw and Galsworthy were still alive and kicking. *Peter Pan* was an annual event, Shaw won the Nobel Prize in 1924 for *Saint Joan*, which, with Sybil Thorndike in the leading role, was the hit of that year and Maugham himself had ten plays performed between 1919 and 1933. There was no doubting the intense excitement generated among the upper classes by the frank exploration of previously taboo subjects – drugs and an immoral older woman in *The Vortex*, drink in *Fallen Angels*, divorce and adultery in *Private Lives*. The plays were a mirror-image of the audience. (There would be little point in going to the theatre otherwise; plays about the lower classes would not be of the slightest interest.) If the mirror-image provided by the polite drawing-room comedies of the past had been very slightly distorted to reveal a seamier side to the lives of the better endowed, well, everyone knew that such things went on. It was just that they had not been mentioned on the stage before.

Above: Sybil Thorndike in Shaw's *Saint Joan* which was the hit of the year in 1924.

Right: Actress Steffi Duna was a huge success in Cochran's production of *Words and Music*.

Shamelessness was in vogue. Freddy Lonsdale achieved a *succès fou* with *Spring Cleaning*, *The Last of Mrs Cheyney*, *On Approval* and, rather more staid, *Maid of the Mountains*. Michael Arlen's *The Green Hat* was turned into a play, with Tallulah Bankhead as the elusive Iris Storm. Basil Dean's dramatization of Margaret Kennedy's *The Constant*

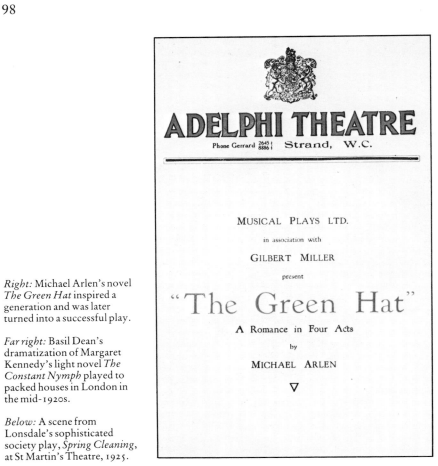

Right: Michael Arlen's novel *The Green Hat* inspired a generation and was later turned into a successful play.

Far right: Basil Dean's dramatization of Margaret Kennedy's light novel *The Constant Nymph* played to packed houses in London in the mid-1920s.

Below: A scene from Lonsdale's sophisticated society play, *Spring Cleaning*, at St Martin's Theatre, 1925.

ST. JAMES'S THEATRE

Sole Lessee ... ... GILBERT MILLER

Under the Management of
GILBERT MILLER
In association with
GERALD DU MAURIER
AND
GLADYS COOPER

"THE LAST OF Mrs. CHEYNEY"
by
FREDERICK LONSDALE

PROGRAMME

MR. GEORGE ALEXANDER.

Far left: Lonsdale's play *The Last of Mrs Cheyney* enjoyed a long run of success in the 1920s.

Left: The old gentlemen actors like Sir George Alexander were ousted in the 1920s by suave and sophisticated playwrights with a penchant for taking the lead role themselves.

Right: Charlie Chaplin in *Modern Times*. He was one of the few silent-screen stars to attract a devoted following among the intelligensia. He became a frequent visitor at Eaton Hall.

Below: Mary Pickford travelled to England in 1924 and was invited to meet the Prince of Wales at a party given in her honour by Mrs Richard Norton. Until the 1920s, only stage actors and actresses had inspired this sort of devotion.

Nymph played to packed houses. Noel Coward played Lewis Dodd, the young composer who very nearly had an adulterous and illegal love affair with the fifteen-year-old Tessa Sanger, only to be saved at the last minute by Tessa's death from consumption. Equally successful was an adaptation of Anita Loos's story of two kept women and their gentlemen friends, *Gentlemen Prefer Blondes*.

The actors and actresses who portrayed these wayward heroes and heroines were as different from the dramatic idols of prewar years as the plays in which they took part. Gone were the tantrums and self-dramatization of Mrs Patrick Campbell, with her guttural voice and her grand manner. Instead actresses fell into various categories. Some were society beauties, like the Countess of Warwick's daughter, Nancy Parsons, and Lady Diana Cooper, whose acting career was silent. Lady Diana appeared in two films, *The Virgin Queen* and *The Glorious Adventure*, and took the part of the Madonna in Max Reinhardt's staging of *The Miracle* at the Lyceum Theatre in 1924. Others were professional beauties, like Gladys Cooper; sultry sex symbols like Tallulah Bankhead; or beautiful talented upstarts, like Gertrude Lawrence, for whom Noel Coward wrote *Private Lives*. Gone, too, was the dignified restraint of the old gentlemen actor-managers such as Sir Herbert Tree, Sir George Alexander or Sir Gerald du Maurier. Noel Coward and Ivor Novello not only acted in other people's plays, they wrote their own, took the leading roles and could sing, dance and write music as well. The jovial entrepreneur C B Cochran not only put on straight plays and cabaret, as well as bringing the Russian Ballet to London, staging cowboy rodeos and introducing the many-ringed circus to Olympia.

Mothers, far from not wanting to put their daughters on the stage, positively encouraged them to become actresses. For the lowborn, there was the possibility of being snatched from the back row of the chorus and whisked off to be mistress of a stately home by an aristocratic admirer – aspirations inflamed by the sight of Rosie Boote disappearing to become Marchioness of Headfort and Gertie Millar marrying the Earl of Dudley. For the highborn, there was the extra allure of public adoration and the heady sound of applause. For the ambitious and talented there were all the trappings of fame and fortune – the gifts of flowers, the champagne, the hampers from Fortnums, as well as the pleasure of being courted by society.

Until the arrival of synchronized-sound pictures in 1927, stage actors and actresses enjoyed a captive market. No-one else could touch them for glamour; they were the apogee of all that was desirable and unattainable. Their clothes, their hair and their movements were slavishly copied by the West End audiences who flocked to their performances. As Barbara Cartland said, 'The stage was very much a part of our life. We went to every new show, we discussed it, criticised it and were absorbed by it. The actors were very real to us. We copied them and tried to look like them.'

Film actors, in the early days of silent films, apart from the odd exception – Douglas Fairbanks Junior (because he was a gentleman) Mary Pickford (because she was a credulous and indestructible china blonde) and Charlie Chaplin (because he played on the heart-strings of the underdog while touching a chord with the intellectually ambitious) – did not produce such a passionate sense of identification. Nevertheless, when they came, the rewards of recognition were sweet. Douglas Fairbanks and Mary Pickford travelled to England in 1924 in considerable state and were invited to meet the Prince of Wales at a party given in their honour by Mrs Richard Norton. The Duke and Duchess of Sutherland asked Mary Pickford to tea and Loelia Ponsonby was so intrigued that she persuaded a friend to hide with her in the garden of the Sutherland mansion in Green Street, so that they would be able to 'peep through the French windows at the tea-party.'

Mary Pickford, for all her undeniable physical charms, was not taken very seriously by what the Duchess of Westminster described euphemistically as 'sophisticated people'. However Charlie Chaplin was taken very seriously, even by 'highbrows', and was 'looked up to as something more than mortal and almost beyond criticism'. A small cockney from Kennington, he became 'King of the Silver Screen', earned more than £150,000 a year and was the most jewelled prize in any hostesses' crown. So, when in 1931 the Duchess learned that he was a fellow passenger on a train from Venice to London she felt faint with nervous anticipation, partly because she was afraid her polite overtures would be rebuffed, and partly because she was worried about the effect he might have on Bendor. She need not have worried. As she wrote later, 'The two of them got on like a house on fire . . . it was a comic little scene, as they both took such immense pains to live up to the other – the Man of the People honoured by the attention of the Duke, and the Duke honoured by the attention of the Great Actor.' It was a game relished by them both and one they never gave up. After that first meeting Chaplin was a frequent guest at Eaton Hall, or at Mimizan for the boar hunting, but he never addressed the Duke in anything other than formal language and Bendor never called him anything but Mr Chaplin.

Despite the excitement of meeting their

Above: Lady Diana Cooper, society beauty, helped make it fashionable for women to appear in films and on the stage. Previously a theatrical career had been considered barely respectable.

102

Right: Kingsway by night. Although the upper classes loved the cinema, they did not dress in their finery as they did for the theatre.

Below: Cinema stars like Fred Astaire and Ginger Rogers enjoyed a huge following and, with the coming of sound to film, they attracted as much or more attention than theatre actors.

idols off the screen, and the novelty that the cinema provided, going to the pictures was never, like the theatre, a means for personal display among the upper classes. Even though picture going had been given the royal seal of approval by the aged Queen Alexandra, who frequently gave exhibitions at Marlborough House, and although two hundred members of the House of Commons had watched a film on the evils of Bolshevism in August 1919, it was not considered necessary to dress to go to the Hammersmith Odeon or the Roxy. Visits were made during the afternoon, before tea. There were no first nights, no white tie or tails, no furs or jewels. There was just the illicit pleasure of sitting in a darkened room unchaperoned, watching Rudolph Valentino pulsating with dark-eyed Latin promise across a flickering desert landscape; or, for the less adventurous, there were a succession of lighthearted romantic suburban comedies – the first glimmer of hope for the inhabitants of Esher that life existed outside the portals of the Ritz and was not confined to the exploits of the aristocracy.

When sound burst onto the celluloid screen in 1927 managements hoped all such snobbish prejudice would melt away. They could now supply everything that the stage had to offer and more. For, suddenly, lips did not just mouth their passions but expressed them in vibrant tones, hooves thudded as they struck the ground, water splashed, glasses clinked and doors slammed open and shut. Instead of a few ill-assorted instrumentalists or a solitary pianist grinding away in the pit, working their way relentlessly through *Tannhauser*, *Aida* or Shubert's *Unfinished Symphony*, whole orchestras throbbed unseen in the background and gleaming Wurlitzer electric organs supplied music during the intervals.

To attract a smarter audience for these fresh delights old cinemas were revamped and new ones built. Vast emporiums like the Tivoli, the Capitol and the Stoll sprang up in the West End, alight with art deco mirrors and complete with bars and refreshment rooms. No expense was spared in the attempt to convince the upper classes that the cinema was not a second-class entertainment. But however much managements tried to woo them, the upper classes continued to cling to their old ways. They went, of course, to see the latest Fred Astaire-Ginger Rogers' dance routine, or Busby Berkeley's spectacular musicals, to swoon over Greta Garbo, Marlene Dietrich or Robert Taylor, and to wallow in the magnificence of the Hollywood sets, but they stubbornly refused to dress to go to the cinema in the evening, while continuing to turn out in full regalia for the theatre.

Hollywood itself exerted a strong fascination. The sight of exotic Moorish palaces, enormous swimming pools, extraordinary bathrooms with sunken baths and Italianate marble halls with cocktail cabinets overflowing with the ingredients for countless variations on an alchoholic theme was a riveting one - particularly as they were entirely inhabited by beautiful, mysterious women and rugged, commanding men. Curiosity about the private lives of these gods and goddesses was insatiable. Their love affairs, their quarrels and their unreasonable demands for money were charted with avid interest by all those who could afford a sixpenny ticket to the cinema. The upper classes, needless to say, went one better. Trips to Beverly Hills to see for themselves became an amusing alternative to Cannes or Nice. Cecil Beaton went and fell in love with Greta Garbo. Noel Coward went too, in 1931 after he had sold the film rights of *Bitter Sweet* to MGM, but at first he found the atmosphere too frenetic. 'I'm not very keen on Hollywood', he wrote home to his mother, 'I'd rather have a nice cup of cocoa, really.'

Later he revised this opinion and was almost, but not quite, seduced by the glamour and the razzmatazz. In 1935, with the film of *Private Lives* a hit at the American box office, and the rights secured for *Cavalcade*, *The Queen was in the Parlour* and *Hay Fever*, he found himself, as he put it, 'the belle of the ball and fêted all ends up.' He was also be-

sieged with offers to stay there permanently, either as a writer of a film star, or both. Metro-Goldwyn Mayer, Twentieth Century Fox and Paramount all competed with each other to lure him into their net. Ceiling-high baskets of flowers, cases of champagne, swimming-pooled mansions, chauffeur-driven Rolls Royces – it was enough to make the most puritanical mouth water. However Noel Coward, although relishing these enticements to the full and enjoying the braggadocio with which they were dangled in front of him, did not succumb.

Instead he went back to England. Soon after he arrived he was summoned to a garden party at Buckingham Palace, in the course of which he reduced the normally staid King George V to helpless laughter. It was recognition of a different sort, but none the less enjoyable for that.

Above: The Capitol Cinema in London's West End. In the 1920s and 1930s cinemas were spectacular affairs, decked out with art deco mirrors and hangings.

Travelling
First Class

Previous page: The Dolly Sisters, girlfriends of the magnate Gordon Selfridge.

The English have always had an ambivalent attitude towards going abroad. A longing to escape to lands where the sun shone all day battled with mistrust of the unsanitary and unpredictable habits of foreigners for supremacy in the Englishman's breast. On the one hand there was the allure of constant warmth, blue seas and fountains of wine and on the other indigestible food and the curious behaviour of those unfortunate enough not to have been born British. It was a knotty problem. One answer was to go to a place so often that part of it lost some of its original and undesirable characteristics and became decently British in outlook. Florence, Venice, Rome, Portofino, Lisbon, Paris, Monte Carlo, Nice, Deauville and Biarritz were all popular for this reason. English tea rooms, English churches with English gravestones, English hospitals, English cows providing English milk, all helped to cushion the expatriate from the worst of an alien land and reassured him that civilization was near at hand.

Another way of avoiding unpleasantness was to travel first class. The rich managed to insulate themselves from the discomfort of draughts, food-poisoning and unpronounceable languages by taking the simple precaution of always going first class. A succession of Pullman carriages, staterooms, private

Below: One of the Duke of Westminster's luxurious yachts moored on the Thames.

yachts and chauffeur-driven cars, manned by an army of valets, ladies' maids, stewards, deckhands and other lackeys, smoothed their path. Loelia, Duchess of Westminster wrote of her travels with Bendor:

I never saw such a thing as a ticket, some minion took care of it. Trains were held up for us, and I even remember an occasion at Euston Station when we arrived just as the express was sliding past the end of the platform, and the station master had it stopped and shunted back again. At Dover and Calais the other passengers were herded aside to allow us to embark and disembark in state across a special gangway. Sometimes during the war when I was sitting on my suitcase in a smokey third class corridor, other human beings wedged tightly against me and my arm aching from having carried my luggage from the car park, I used to remember what it was like travelling with Bendor.

The first journey the Duchess made in these luxurious circumstances was soon after she became engaged, in 1925, when she accompanied her fiancé on a shooting trip to Albania. They began by taking the Golden Arrow to Paris, and continued on the night train to Venice, where one of the Duke's yachts, the *Flying Cloud*, was waiting to take them across the Adriatic and down the Dalmation coast. Bendor refused to answer any of his bride-to-be's questions about money, tickets or suitable clothes (was it hot or cold in Albania?)

only telling her to be at Victoria Station at a certain time with 'whatever she chose to pack and a passport'. From then on she was whisked through the looking-glass into a world peopled by benevolent genies, who appeared and disappeared at their master's bidding with miraculous speed and whose sole purpose was to gratify his every whim. Bendor, too, seemed to have magical powers. In Paris they spent a few hours in the permanent suite the Duke kept in the Hotel Lotti.

Above: The English abroad felt able to let their hair down. Here tourists at Deauville, France, play Kiss in the Ring, 1924.

Below: The all-white Pullman The Golden Arrow began its express run from Calais to Paris in 1926, offering passengers every comfort.

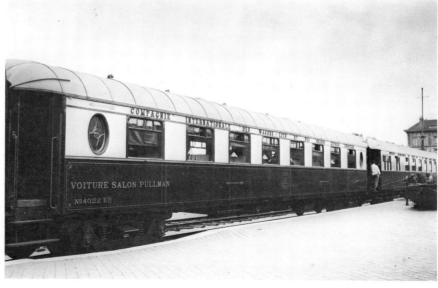

Above: Passengers recline in the Social Hall of the *Leviathan* in 1923. This and other photographs were found in a secret panel marked 'X' on the photograph.

often draughty establishments. A central heating system, based on hot water from the low-pressure boiler, and teak and mahogany panelling on the walls insulated and warmed the rooms, which were lit by huge gas chandeliers. The waiters in the dining room wore powdered wigs, tail coats, breeches and silk stockings, the tables were laid with white damask cloths, silver knives and forks and glasses of Baccarat crystal and the menus stretched even the most hardy Victorian digestion to the limit – the first dinner consisted of ten courses and lasted for three hours.

Although the First World War put an end to much of the old grandeur, there were still enough of the old delights, and some new ones, to tempt the discerning traveller. The number of courses at dinner might have been cut to five, but the company still employed a French chef to titillate the palate. The gas chandeliers might have been changed to side lighting, but the heating system still worked efficiently and it was relaxing to be able to have a bath in one of the new bath cars.

Eventually, festooned with jewels and in a haze of romantic bliss, which even a thick Venetian fog could not dispel, the newly engaged pair boarded the *Flying Cloud*. There, as far as the Duchess was concerned, the idyll came to an abrupt end. It was not that the Duke had suddenly shed his mask of magnificence, but that she was sea-sick. 'It really was an irony of fate', she wrote, 'that I should become part-owner of two enormous yachts, capable of sailing on any ocean and not be able to spend a happy moment on either. . . . I had only to step on board and I immediately felt queasy. One whiff of engine oil and all was lost.'

It was, indeed, a pity, for the *Flying Cloud* was as extravagant and outlandish as everything else belonging to Bendor. Rated as one of the thirty largest yachts in the world, with a length of 203.5 feet and a gross tonnage of 1178.74, she was an auxiliary twin-screw four-masted schooner, built at Leghorn in 1927. The upper cabins were reached through an ornamental doorway, designed to look like the front door of a Cotswold house. Inside, the cabins were panelled in oak or pine and furnished with small-scale Queen Anne furniture. The room allocated to the Duchess had a four-poster bed with hangings of embroidered Florentine silk. As she said, '. . . when stationary, one could almost believe that one was in a private house in England.'

Unfortunately for Loelia, the Duke had no sooner set foot on board than he wanted to sail for the open sea and, once there, the rougher the weather the better. He was an excellent sailor and greatly enjoyed rolling waves, furious winds and the excitement of

Fortified by oysters and champagne, Loelia went up to her room to fetch her felt hat before leaving for the train. Pinned to it she found a large diamond clip. Later more glittering objects fell into her hands. In her suitcase she discovered a platinum powder box studded with diamonds and sapphires; in her sleeper she was woken up by a hard lump that materialized into a diamond and emerald brooch; and next morning, at breakfast, when they arrived at the frontier, she opened her handbag to get out her passport and saw a diamond and ruby bracelet with a long diamond tassle inside.

Apart from the excitement of these surprises there was the pleasure of travelling on the Arlberg Orient Express. Maybe it was not quite as it had been in 1883, when what has been described as a 'land liner' and a 'grand hotel on wheels' set out on its maiden voyage from Paris to the Bosphorous. Then the amazed passengers found they had stepped from the platform into an elaborately appointed series of replicas of a French *château*, a London club and an Italian *palazzo*, but with none of the discomfort and inconvenience associated with these large and battling against the elements. As even Bendor's powers did not extend to commanding the spirits of the deep, his desire for this entertainment was often frustrated by calm waters and cloudless skies. The sea was no respecter of persons.

Nevertheless, the rich who took to the water, whether they were in a sailing yacht, a steam yacht or crossing the Atlantic in a liner, were outraged if their enjoyment was spoilt by anything as inconvenient as change in the weather. Lady Diana Cooper, whose husband was appointed First Lord of the Admiralty in 1937, found herself mistress of the sloop *Enchantress*. In September of that year, together with some friends, she set sail full of anticipation for the Western Isles, 'complete with yachting caps, Royal Squadron badges and buttons,' only to run into squally weather within three days. She wrote gloomily to her friend Conrad Russell:

By 3.30 the tide was rolling hysterically and I was bathed in sweat. It was only with difficulty that I kept myself from seeking help. Suddenly there was a super-roll, followed by a series of crashes, and I leapt up and dashed into Duff's cabin opposite. What should I find but a scene of chaos! The bed had "got away" from its mooring, the whole of the bedding, mattress, blankets, pillows on the floor in a tangle and poor Duff picking himself up, bruised and bewildered. . . .

Left: Cruises were a popular form of travel in the 1920s. All the comforts of home could be found along with the exotica of far-away places.

Much the same thing happened to the Bright Young Things in Evelyn Waugh's *Vile Bodies*. They had set out to cross the Atlantic with high hopes of sipping cocktails at the first-class bar, drinking champagne at the Captain's table and meeting really important

Below: A group of passengers visit the bridge of the *Aquitania*, the largest floating ballroom, during a masked county ball in 1927.

Above: A dance aboard the Cunard liner SS *Berengaria* in aid of the Southampton Children's Hospital in April 1929. The upper classes often managed to combine charity and fun.

people (like last week's Prime Minister, the Right Honourable Walter Outrage), only to find that everything was spoilt by the prospect of bad weather – a phenomenon none of them could do anything about. When the inevitable happened and the ship rolled and pitched and swayed up and down, the cries of amazement and self-pity were unbounded. ('Oh', said the Bright Young People, 'Oh, oh, oh'.)

Storms at sea sometimes provided compensations for the strong-stomached. Isolated from their weaker brethren, the survivors drew together in communal friendship and in the battered staterooms and empty dining rooms, barriers of class and sex broke down. 'But for this we might never have met', said an unknown man to Charles Ryder and Julia Mottram in *Brideshead Revisited*, after the expected hurricane had turned the liner into a deserted ship, adding: 'I've had some very romantic encounters at sea in my time.' Later, posing as husband and wife, they went to a 'get-together party', where they drank champagne with eighteen people, who had 'nothing in common except immunity from seasickness.' The next day, thrown once more into each other's company and released from the necessity of observing the usual preliminaries of flirtation and courtship, they went to bed in Julia's cabin.

Neither Charles Ryder nor Julia Mottram, both characters who took themselves extremely seriously, would have put the consummation of the great love of their lives down to anything as mundane as availability in unfamiliar surroundings. But, as Paul Fussell rightly pointed out, 'making love in novel environments, free from the censorship and inhibitions of the familiar, is one of the

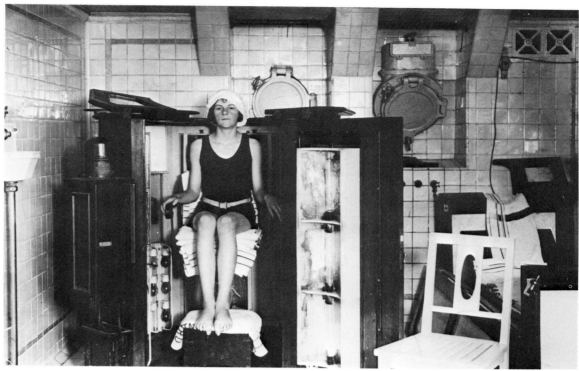

headiest of travel promises.' Julia Mottram had some inkling of this when she asked plaintively, 'Where can we hide in fair weather, we orphans of the storm?', and certainly Mrs Ardwinkle in Aldous Huxley's *Those Barren Leaves*, understood the temptations perfectly. Travelling with the poet Chelifer, she hoped to predispose him in her favour by exposing him to the romantic delights of the Appian Way at sunset, and the Colosseum by moonlight, observing wryly and with some truth that '. . . more proposals are made . . . in the face of an impressive view, within the labyrinth of a ruined palace, than in the drab parlours or the streets of West Kensington.'

Illicit love away from home was not the sole prerogative of the rich, but there is no doubt that the more forbidden fruits of passion were able to be satisfied with greater ease by those who could afford to travel at whim. How else could E M Forster's Miss Quested have managed to go to India and have such a disturbing experience in the Marabar caves, or Christopher Isherwood, Wystan Auden and Stephen Spender uncover so many seedy haunts of male eroticism in Berlin, or Norman Douglas indulge his pederastic urges in Italy and France? How else could Somerset Maugham set up house with Gerald Haxton in Cap Ferrat, or Nancy Cunard with her black lover in Paris? Quite apart from the inconvenient and inhibiting laws governing sexual behaviour in England, the social and intellectual climate was not conducive to such

Above: A woman takes a Turkish bath aboard the SS *Berengaria* in July 1923. Luxury liners could offer all the facilities of a large hotel as well as the excitement of life on board ship.

Left: Some 200 couples attended the charity ball aboard the *Aquitania*, docked at Southampton. A group of partygoers lounge on the ship's swimming pool.

Left and below: The luxurious splendour of the Ritz Hotel, Paris. The English avoided the discomfort of travelling abroad by going first class all the way.

exotic aberrations. It was only across the channel that they could flourish undisturbed.

Extravagances of all kinds awaited those who did. Kings and Princes in and out of exile and emigré Russian Grand Dukes stalked the Riviera, and Laura Corrigan and Elsa Maxwell staged exuberantly lavish parties in Venice, as Nancy Cunard wrote to Norman Douglas:

The whole hectic spin of Venice in the twenties, all the more exotic on account of its cosmopolitanism . . . the petty intrigues and funny scandals: balls and fancy dress galas and festivities . . . that blazing Lido strewn with society stars in glittering jewels and make-up – that brilliance of Grand Canal Barge-Parties – those spontaneous dawn revels after dancing in some of the rather sinister new night-bars. A time when everyone thought everyone else crazy.

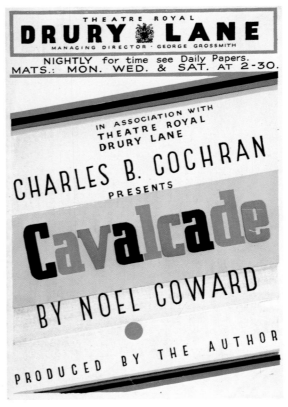

Above and far left below: Fancy dress parties thrown by The Bright Young Things in the 1920s were heavily featured in contemporary magazines.

Above left: The stage adaptation of Margaret Kennedy's novel *The Constant Nymph* played to packed houses.

Left: Noel Coward was the most popular playwright of the 1920s.

Right: Dame Edith Sitwell, painted by Alvaro Guevara, one of the first contributors to Nancy Cunard's Hours Press.

Left: A caricature of some of the visitors to the Derby in 1934. The Aga Khan is centre, talking to the jockey.

Right: A hand-tinted photograph of Mrs Freda Dudley Ward, one of the Prince of Wales' companions, taken by Bassano, from the *Sketch* in 1922.

Below: Crowds watch the races at Ascot in 1920, one of the most famous sporting occasions in England, and an excuse for the rich to show off new fashions, particularly in hats.

Left: A cartoon depicts boaters at Deauville. The South of France became a popular summer resort in the 1920s.

Overleaf: Cleopatra's Needle and Hungerford Bridge from the Savoy, painted by C R W Nevinson *c* 1924.

Left: Arrival of the Jarrow Marchers, 1936, by T C Dugdale, exemplifies the divide between rich and poor during the Depression.

Right: By the 1920s the ritual of wintering in Switzerland was well-established among the rich.

Far right: Visits to the ballet, along with the opera and theatre, were a feature of the Season in London.

Below: At the Casino, a painting by René Vincent which appeared in the *Tatler* in 1922.

Winter Sports
Season 1923-4
THOS. COOK & SON.

Above: The Embassy Club was one of London's most popular nightspots of the 1920s.

Left: Fancy dress balls had become so popular in the 1920s that Bovril used this party scene for an advertisement.

Far left: A fancy dress costume designed by Miss Dolly Tree.

Right: Two young ladies discuss the problems of trying to fit all their invitations into their diary.

A VIGNETTE
of the LONDON
SEASON, 1931

**From a Drawing
in Colour ⸗ ⸗ by
HOOKWAY COWLES**

SYLVIA: It ought to be a good party. Lady Ted usually gets a cheery crowd. And her cook—my dear, Quaglino!

ROSE: But what about Wimbledon? George may be in the finals of the Mixed.

SYLVIA: You can get up for that. They'll lend you the Bentley.

ROSE: Then there's Vi's bridge, and Gerald was going to take me to the Embassy Ball.

SYLVIA: Darling, you're *too* popular. I wish I had half your invitations.

ROSE: Would you say "yes" to all of them, darling?

Above: Life at Monte Carlo as drawn by Claude Shepperson. The wealthy enjoyed the more relaxed style of life possible on the Continent.

Right: Two London Transport posters advertise the entertainments available to the less well-off.

Far right: Crowds dressed in their evening finery pour into Shaftesbury Avenue, London, after a night at the theatre.

UNDERGROUND

FOR THE SUNDAY CONCERTS

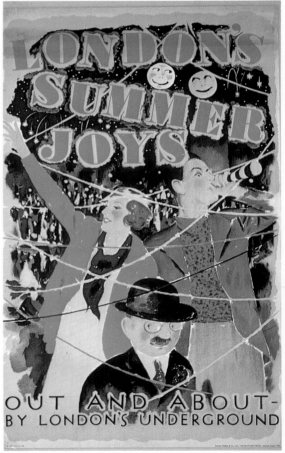

LONDON'S SUMMER JOYS

OUT AND ABOUT— BY LONDON'S UNDERGROUND

LONDON PRIDE

Left: A view over the Thames, looking towards the Houses of Parliament.

Right: Lady Ottoline Morrell, painted by Simon Bussy. She gathered around her many of London's leading artists and intellectuals in the 1920s.

Below: Fancy dress costumes featured in the *Sketch* in 1928. These balls were so popular that the *Sketch* ran a competition for the best designs.

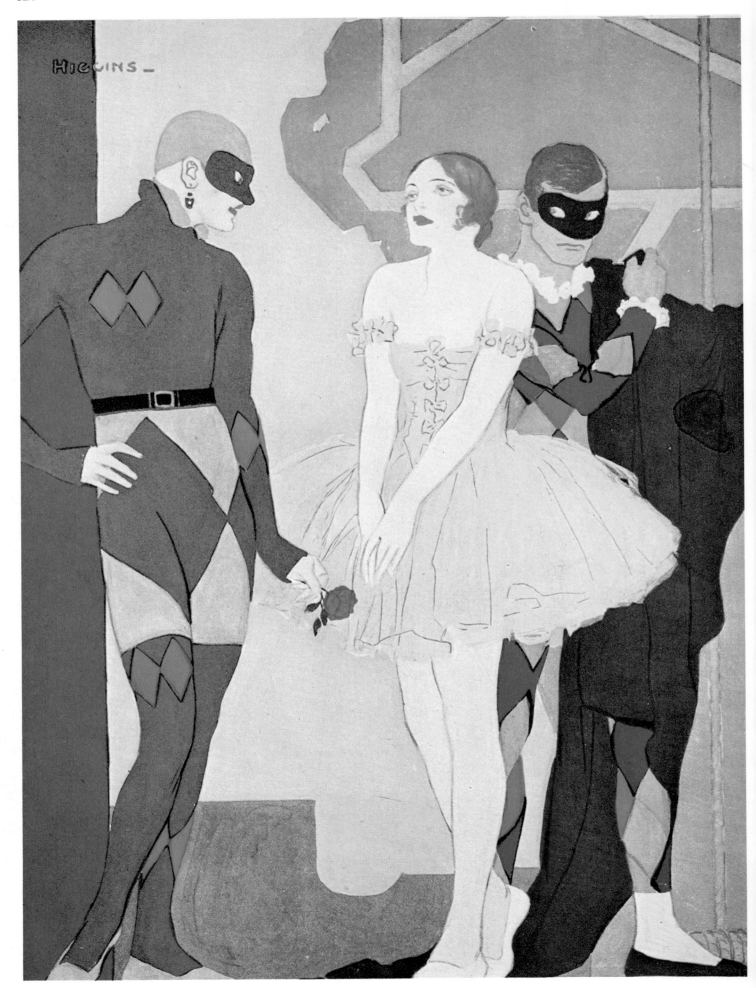

Left: Two harlequins and a ballerina at a ball in the 1920s.

Bottom: Scott and Zelda Fitzgerald with their daughter Mollie at Antibes in 1926. They shocked the French with their outrageous behaviour.

Below: American bathers enjoy the sunshine at Deauville in August 1922. Previously a winter resort, the Murphys started the habit of visiting the Riviera during the summer.

There were free drinks at the the Grand Hotel or Lido bar for all Laura Corrigan's guests at the Grand Hotel. Lady Diana Cooper, who stayed there in August 1931 wrote:

It's all a modern fairy story, with everything that Beauty wants in her new palace, twenty backgammon boards, rare friandise, and, since there are flesh-and-blood servants and many of them, placards on all the bedroom tables warn you to tip them at their peril, and whatever we do we mustn't buy stamps or cigarettes, or pay for washing or cleaning, or coiffures. . . .

On the Cote d'Azure in the summer of 1922 two rich expatriate Americans, Gerald and Sara Murphy, rented the entire ground floor of the Grand Hotel du Cap d'Antibes for themselves and their friends. This in itself was

something of an innovation. Nobody went to the Riviera between March and October. But, even more extraordinary, the Murphys had an unnatural desire to lie in the sun. As this odd fad was not catered for by the hotel, which did not have a beach in front of it, they decided to build themselves a villa behind the tiny seaweed-infested beach of la Garoupe. Under the curious eyes of the local inhabitants, who thought them very peculiar indeed, they removed the weed and spent the next few months lying on the white sand which lay beneath, covered with banana oil and turning an unfashionable brown.

The trail having been blazed, others came to sample the delights of the Riviera out of season. Rudolph Valentino, Cole Porter and Ernest Hemingway came to stay and, in 1924, Scott and Zelda Fitzgerald left Paris and rented a villa nearby, at St Raphael. Once there, with the brilliant blue sea to cool them from the heat, exotic food to eat, a never-ending supply of wine and with the scent of lemon, orange, pine and eucalyptus in their nostrils, they prepared to taste the fruits of paradise.

In 1924 the Fitzgeralds were both under thirty and at the height of their confidence and physical powers. Zelda's golden hair shone in the sun and her eyes slanted with promise. Scott had written *The Great Gatsby*, which had been received with respectful admiration by his fellow writers. Gertrude Stein told Scott he was 'creating a contemporary world much as Thackeray did'; T S Eliot

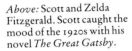
Above: Scott and Zelda Fitzgerald. Scott caught the mood of the 1920s with his novel *The Great Gatsby*.

Above right: A bathing belle at Deauville, August 1924. It became fashionable to acquire a tan in the 1920s.

said that he had taken the first step in American fiction since Henry James; and Gilbert Seldes, writing in the American literary magazine, *The Dial*, was convinced that he had 'more than matured' and had 'mastered his talents and gone soaring in a beautiful flight, leaving behind him everything dubious and tricky in his earlier work.... leaving behind all the men of his own generation and most of his elders.'

They were a formidable pair. Gerald Murphy described them as a pair of conspirators:

They would begin in the evening . . . you would see some look come over them as though they had been drawn together . . . then they were inseparable . . . it was as though they were waiting for something to happen; they seemed to be looking forward to something fantastic. That's the only way I can put it; something had to happen, something extravagant.

The high jinks that followed these conspiratorial glances were often disconcerting for the unprepared French *habitués* of the cafés and bars they frequented. One night Zelda danced alone at the Casino at Juan-les Pins, watched by a crowd of gaping Frenchmen, as she slowly lifted her skirts above her waist and swayed rhythmically to the strains of the small orchestra. One time they threw a farewell party at Eden Roc for Alexander Woolcott, Grace Moore and Chato Elizaga. 'A great many toasts were drunk', wrote Christopher Matthew, 'and a great many speeches made, until finally Zelda Fitzgerald shouted, "Words, mere words. Can't we give our friends a real present , like this?" ' Whereupon, he added, she leapt onto a chair, whipped off her panties, and threw them at Elizaga. He, not to be outdone by this gesture, bowed gravely at Zelda and vaulted over the balcony fully clothed into the sea. After that Alexander Woolcott took all his clothes off and marched into the hotel, through the lobby and up to his room.'

Occasionally Zelda's behaviour was destructive as well as exhibitionist, and her acts of bravado verged on the suicidal. She challenged Scott to diving competitions off the rocks by night, climbing higher and higher until they were thirty feet above the water, relying on their sense of timing to save them from hitting the rocks below. In 1925, while dining at an inn two hundred feet above a valley at St-Paul-de-Vence, Zelda felt Scott was paying too much attention to Isadora Duncan, sitting at a nearby table. Before the incredulous eyes of the diners, she got up and jumped down a stone stairwell on the edge of the terrace, appearing a few minutes later covered with blood.

Scott showed little sign of emotion. Neither of them, according to Zelda, believed in 'conservation'. Life must never be allowed to become a losing game and if flirting with death stacked the odds in their favour, then it was a game worth playing. Certainly there was never any question in either of their minds that to be was not enough. To exist in the present was the only thing that mattered.

The Murphys and the Fitzgeralds did not have the Riviera to themselves for long. Within a few years the floodgates opened. By 1930 the sight of basking bodies had become commonplace, and hotels rushed to provide cocktail bars, dance floors and outdoor restaurants to cater for the insatiable demands of a steady stream of sun worshippers, eager for dry martinis and night life. The manufacture of beachwear became a thriving industry – the Italian designer Shiaparelli made vivid beach dresses and shorts in shocking pinks and purples and Vera Boren produced pyjama suits 'with flared trousers and neat double-breasted linen jackets to wear with a spotted silk scarf and a jaunty little sailor's cap or a large floppy hat.' The Eden Roc pavilion was lined daily with what Scott Fitzgerald described as 'notable and fashionable' people, English as well as

American, and the glossy magazines spared no effort to obtain pictures of the smart set at play. In 1930 the *Graphic* showed 'an attractive glimpse of Eden Roc at Cap D'Antibes, the summer rendezvous on the Riviera where many well-known English people gather to lunch and bathe in the sun', and noticed that Lady Ashley, Mr Cecil Beaton (in a French *matelot* outfit), the Marchioness of Milford Haven, Miss Tallulah Bankhead (seen repairing her make-up), Beatrice Lillie, Noel Coward and Bernard Shaw were all indulging in these pleasurable activities.

If they were not staying at the Grand Hotel du Cap, or at the Carlton, whose twin domes at each extremity were said to have been modelled on the breasts of a 'famous beauty' –

MARIEGOLD AT EDEN ROC!
1. *Mariegold found a fierce controversy raging among the devastatingly nude occupants of Eden Roc—the oldest and most select inhabitants (or "Coal Black Mammy" school of thought) fiercely resenting—*

2. *—the intrusion of mere upstart, half-baked "Chocolate Kids."*

3. *While the new school of "Curry" (introduced by Colonel Sblud Grillyer) was considered only less reprehensible than the new arrivals' objectionable shade of Lobster!*

Above: The *Sketch* in 1932 pokes gentle fun at the new fashion for lying in the sun.

THE TATLER   [No. 1729, AUGUST 15, 1934

ON THE BLUE COAST

AT EDEN ROC: MRS. NUGENT HOPE

AT CAP D'ANTIBES: MR. WILLIAM BURTON, MR. DEREK STUDLEY-HERBERT AND MR. GUY CARLETON-PAGET

MRS. GUY CARLETON-PAGET

AT CAP D'ANTIBES: MR AND MRS. CHARLES FARRELL

AT EDEN ROC: THE COUNTESS OF SEAFIELD

AT MONTE CARLO: MR. AND MRS. HARRY HAYES MORGAN

In this page are some of the advance guard of the autumn emigrants to one of the few places on the Continent where they have not got the machine-gun habit. The Blue Coast is both peaceful and sunny—a shining example, in fact, to some other spots on the map. Of those in this little gallery Mrs. Nugent Hope is the wife of Captain Nugent Hope, who hunts his own private pack in Herefordshire. Mr. Derek Studley-Herbert and his wife, Lady Seafield, are staying with Mr. William Burton, the American artist and yachtsman, who is very busy painting at his villa at Mougins. Mr. and Mrs. Guy Carleton-Paget are on their honeymoon. She is Major and Mrs. J. B. Paget's daughter, and her husband assumed the additional name of Paget just before the wedding. Mr. Charles Farrell, one of Hollywood's greatest, needs no introduction. Mr. and Mrs. Harry Hayes Morgan, who are at Monte, are racing a boat during the coming regatta week. He is a brother of Thelma Lady Furness, and was elected President of the Cresta Tobogganing Club when the Hon. Francis Curzon became Hon. Life-President

Left: The *Tatler* features some foreign visitors to the French Riviera in 1934.

Right: The Dolly Sisters accompanied their protector, Mr Selfridge, to Monte Carlo and soon ran up huge bills at the casinos.

Below: Mrs Murray enjoys a morning bathe at the beginning of the season at Deauville, 1926.

a cryptic allusion which gave more than one well-endowed lady reason for hope – the members of this élite bought, built or rented their own villas, or stayed aboard one of the many private yachts that jostled for harbour space along the coast. An ex-Duchess of Marlborough occupied a villa surounded by cypress trees that had a view from Cannes to Rapallo; Somerset Maugham turned the Villa Mauresque into a voluptuous Moorish *hacienda* and filled it with Siamese bronzes, Spanish baroque furniture and French Impressionist paintings; and Michael Arlen drove his enormous yellow speedboat, *Swallow 2*, through the water beneath his hillside villa at Cannes.

Gone was the wildness and the strangeness of the Côte d'Azure of five years before. Private affluence had been replaced by public display. It was no longer Zelda Fitzgerald's black-foliaged Provence, with 'clouds of moths whipping the heliotrope dusk, where people do not need to see unless they are looking for the nightingale', but a glittering nickel-and-chrome-plated temple of luxury. The brashness of magnates like Gordon Selfridge, who had loaded his girlfriends, the two Dolly sisters, so heavily with diamonds that they staggered as they made their entrance into the Casino, had spilled over from Monte Carlo and invaded the whole coast.

The Dolly sisters, who had begun their career in cabaret at the Kit Kat Club in London, found no difficulty in adjusting to their new circumstances. Their besotted protector not only covered them with jewels from head to foot, he indulged their passion for gambling, even going so far as to buy an interest in the Casino at Le Touquet so that Jenny could have unlimited credit - a facility she used to the full, often winning or losing £100,000 in a night. When even the open-handed Mr Selfridge was drained dry and was unable to settle an outstanding debt of £90,000, Jenny committed suicide, thus, as one commentator put it laconically, depriving the casino of a 'very good customer'.

Casinos, however, could and did survive without Gordon Selfridge. At Deauville the baccarat table took a minimum stake of $175 and was surrounded nightly by a band of hopeful gamblers of various nationalities intent on accumulating wealth by overtly entrepreneurial means. That Mr Solly Joel, the financier, and racehorse owners, Lord Furness, Lord Carnarvon and the Sultan of Jahore, sat alongside the wily Nicolas Zographos (so-called leader of a Greek gambling syndicate who, it was maintained, had once won F9 million on two cards at baccarat, and lost F36 million in one week at Monte Carlo; and who in 1939 was said to be worth 'anything between £10 and £50 million), was a matter for congratulation on the part of the investors.

It was not only gambling that attracted the visitors to the north coast of France. Parisians preferred the sandy beaches of Deauville, Le Touquet and Cabourg to the unknown hazards of Biarritz or Juan-les-Pins. Apart from the beaches, there was *le sport*, racing at Deauville, polo at le Touquet, as well as tennis and golf. The English often found a weekend in Normandy a more attractive prospect than a damp Saturday to Monday in Leicestershire, particularly as, by the early 1930s, they could take an aeroplane from Croydon airport to le Touquet (or, even more daring, pilot their own) across the channel in a matter of hours.

Above: (left to right) Gerald Haxton, Lady Leon, Somerset Maugham and Leovald the 'professional' at Cap Ferrat.

The more intrepid could fly further afield. Crossing the Atlantic by air was still in its infancy; by 1930 only about a hundred people had made the journey in airships. No more of these floating airliners were produced after October 1930, when the British-built *R 101* crashed near Beauvais on its maiden flight to India, burning to death all those on board, including Lord Thompson, the Labour Air Minister. Nevertheless, the glamour and excitement surrounding solo fliers such as Charles Lindbergh, Amy Johnson and Amelia Earhart had made the Imperial Airways' flights to Paris, Amsterdam, Brussels and Vienna increasingly popular for those able to withstand the unpredictable behaviour of the small aeroplanes, which were liable to shudder and bump about in good weather as well as bad. Cecil Beaton flew to Amsterdam and, although extremely nervous, felt it was a 'modern and commendable thing' to have done; and the Prince of Wales flew to Vienna for the skiing at Kitzbühl, an activity and a resort he did much to make fashionable.

The ritual of the annual winter skiing holiday, now firmly entrenched in upper-class minds as the part of the year they would least like to have to give up in times of economic stringency, was, in the 1920s and early 1930s, more a pursuit for the adventurous and athletic than the socially ambitious. Skating could be enjoyed anywhere that the ice was sound enough and provided the added thrill of skimming over the ice to the strains of the latest foxtrot, but skiing required more of its participants. Before the introduction of drag lifts and cable cars, there was the laborious busi-

134

SWITZERLAND RESUMING ITS RÔLE AS A PLAYGROUND OF EUROPE: BRITISH

PHOTOGRAPHS BY SPORT AND GENERAL.

WINTER SPORTS AT ST. MORITZ: A TYPICAL SCENE ON THE VILLAGE TOBOGGAN RUN.

SKI-ING IN A SNOWSTORM: MISS BARBARA LUTYENS, LADY ALEXANDRA CURZON, AND MR. MICHAEL TENNANT AT MÜRREN.

YOUNG ENGLAND IN SWITZERLAND: THE MISSES SYBIL EGERTON, WITH THEIR TOBOGGANS, AT M

SOCIETY AT MÜRREN: LORD LYTTON (ON THE RIGHT, AT THE BACK) AND HIS PARTY ON THE ICE.

SKATING AT MÜRREN: CAPT. ERIC MACKENZIE, SC AND MISS BARBARA LUTYENS.

ONE OF THE BEST ENGLISH SKATERS IN THE CONTINENTAL STYLE: LORD LYTTON.

SKI-ING AT MÜRREN: LADY CYNTHIA CURZON, SECOND DAUGHTER OF EARL CURZON.

THE G.O.C. OF LONDON'S AIR DEFENCES AT MÜRREN: GEN ASHMORE AND MRS. ASHMORE ON THE RINK.

LORD L HERMIO

Many people well known in British Society have been enjoying the revived opportunities for winter sports in Switzerland this season. The Earl of Lytton, who is himself one of the best of English skaters in the Continental style, has been entertaining a party at Mürren, where his elder son, Viscount Knebworth, who is only sixteen, won the Visitors' ski-ing race. Lady Lytton had the pleasure of presenting the prize to him. The group shown in one of the above photographs (the left-hand one of the two in the centre) includes the following - reading from left to right: Capt. Eric MacKenzie, Miss Barbara Lutyens, Colquhoun, Bt., and Lady Hermione Lytton. Major - General E. since 1917. Earlier in the war he commanded a Brigade of the

All pictures: Skiing, skating and tobogganing in the early 1920s. Before the introduction of drag lifts, skiing was a sport enjoyed by the adventurous and athletic rather than the socially ambitious. Skiers tended to wear functional clothes, while skaters were able to indulge their taste for elegant furs and velvets.

ness of struggling back up the slope – a twenty-minute downhill run meant a morning's climb on sealskins. Such mortification of the flesh was not to everyone's taste, and those who responded to the challenge tended to wear appropriately functional clothes: khaki breeches or baggy trousers. Skiers were given to displays of heartiness and moral superiority, in sharp contrast to the skaters, who dressed in furs and velvet and who exuded an aura of elegance, romance and sexual promise.

Davos and Zermatt were the first resorts to install some form of uphill transport. Davos

had the Parsenn railway and Zermatt a ratchet train called the Grannie, which took an hour and a half to labour up to Gornergrat, but these were originally built to attract summer, not winter, visitors. It was not until 1931, when a Swiss engineer, Gerhard Muller, invented the drag lift and so made it possible to do a run every ten minutes, that skiing shed its earnest image and acquired a more light-hearted one. By the end of 1938, with the first cable cars in operation at most major resorts, and hotels catering for an influx of enthusiasts, ski fever became rampant.

...S ENJOYING WINTER SPORTS.

A POPULAR CENTRE OF WINTER SPORTS IN THE ENGADINE: ST. MORITZ A GENERAL VIEW OF THE RAILWAY STATION.

...AUGHTER: LADY ...I AT MÜRREN.

ONLY CHILD OF LORD ISLINGTON: THE HON. JOAN DICKSON-POYNDER SKI-ING.

...Viscount Knebworth, Lady Cynthia Curzon, Lady Alexandra Curzon, the Earl of Lytton, Sir Ian ...e central photograph below, has been General Officer Commanding the Air Defences of London ...e is a daughter of the Rev. F. W. Parsons, Vicar of Tandridge, Surrey.

In the wake of ski fever came après-ski fever. At the Palace Hotel in St Moritz were seen what were said to be the most beautiful women in the world, 'sparkling with diamonds, their furs as crisp as the mountain air outside, shimmered cheek to cheek round the dance floor with men whose profiles were as well-publicised as their names. . . .' At Megève there was a hotel designed especially for skiers, called La Residence du Sporting, where Madame Shiaparelli was to be found 'drifting around in wonderful evening dresses'. At the Hotel du Mont Blanc Cocteau

painted murals on the walls in case visiting Parisians should suffer from cultural withdrawal symptoms.

Yearnings for Paris were not confined to the French. The English and the Americans also found it agreeable. Barriers of language melted away before the delights it had to offer. There were the cabarets round the Place Pigalle, Mistinguette still flaunting her feathers at the Folies Bergères, Josephine Baker singing at the Casino de Paris and countless interesting little cafés on the left bank. There was the sensuous beauty of the city itself, described by Harold Acton in his memoirs: 'The Seine under the stars, the narrow streets jutting off at curious angles into the darkness . . . the multiple bridges with their mysterious arches, the parks locked up, only ponds and plants alive there, assuming marvellous dream shapes under the moon. . .' Above all there was the liberation from the artistic and sexual restraints that hemmed them in at home.

Once in Paris, copies of *Lady Chatterley's Lover*, *Ulysses* and *The Well of Loneliness* could be released from their plain brown covers, lovers of all inclinations could hold hands in broad daylight and dabbling in drugs and drinking to excess were not frowned on. For a few francs a day life could be led to the brink of self-destruction. 'In a minute we will break our necks', wrote Prosper Merimée, 'but how splendid one feels in the air!'

Not everyone approved of such wilful per-

sonal abuse. Gertrude Stein complained to Ernest Hemingway that he was one of a 'lost generation' with 'no respect for anything' and that he would drink himself to death. Hemingway, in his turn, tried to prevent Scott Fitzgerald from drinking more than eight whiskies and two bottles of champagne a day and Ford Madox Ford advised Hemingway not to drink brandy. 'Don't you know', he said, 'it's fatal for a young writer to drink brandy?' Harold Acton also found the drinking habits of the Bohemian Americans of Montparnasse difficult to stomach, but put them down to the fact that they were less intellectually conscious than the French, and so required coarser stimulants. Neither did he have a very great opinion of their writings, which he dismissed as the 'product of their next-day hangovers'. He observed in his memoirs:

Hemingway, Ezra Pound, Ford Madox Ford, pontificated more or less among bevies of truculent women. It was considered essential to look tough, to simulate the cowboy, if only in flourishing verbal lassoos, to make a cult of the

Above: Cabaret star Josephine Baker was one of the many delights Paris had to offer in the 1920s.

Left: Skiers wend their way up the slopes at St Moritz in 1924 before the introduction of drag lifts.

138

Hay. In 1926, having published her first book of poems *Outlaws*, she finally came to rest on the Île de St Louis.

There she began to be her 'real self'. She also got her own back on her mother by luring the aged George Moore into her net, asking his advice about her poetry, having him to dinner and feeding his carnal fantasies with promises to take her clothes off and show herself to him. When she actually did so he was beside himself with delight: 'Oh! What a beautiful back you have, Nancy, it is as long as a weasel's. What a beautiful back.'

Tantalizing her mother's old admirer was only the beginning. Poor Lady Cunard had to put up with Nancy's strange friends, too. At first they were the sort she herself had always encouraged – young French writers and painters such as Jean Cocteau, Louis Aragon and Paul Chirico, and older ones like Marie Laurençin and André Dérain. When Nancy bought a house outside Paris and began to print her friends' works herself under the imprint of the Hours Press, her mother was full of advice and support. The list of the first eight contributors was impeccable: George Moore, Ezra Pound, Richard Aldington, Norman Douglas, Iris Tree, Alvaro Guevara and Louis Aragon. Lady Cunard could not have done better herself.

In 1930, however, rumours began to reach her that Nancy had been to Venice and come back with a black jazz pianist. Shudders of distaste ran up and down Lady Cunard's spine; to live openly with a negro lover did not come into the realms of possibility. It smacked of excess. It was not respectable at

hair upon your chest . . . How little they assimilated from their sojourn in France! They seldom penetrated French life beyond the aperitif stage. As writers they flourished under borrowed plumes, the prestige of Paris as an art capital, which they forgot was due to the genius of the French. . . .

An expatriate who assimilated herself completely into French life was Nancy Cunard. Driven out of London by the merciless competitiveness of her mother, Nancy decided to make a life for herself in Paris and write poetry. In 1920 she made a tentative move across the channel, and was immortalized by novelists – as Iris in Michael Arlen's *Green Hat* and as Mrs. Viveash in Aldous Huxley's *Antic*

THE LADY OF THE BROBDINGNAGIAN BANGLES: MISS NANCY CUNARD.

SMOKING

all. That Henry Crowder was perfectly respectable and quite as hesitant about the whole situation as Lady Cunard was not taken into account, he was an alien predator and as such should be shunned and reviled.

Nancy not only associated with undesirable people, she also caused a scandal by arranging a private screening in London of a film by Luis Bunũel and Salvador Dali that had caused an uproar in Paris. *L'Age d'Or*, a surrealist fantasy, had the two main ingredients for public seizure; blasphemy and sex. The combination of these two sins against society was too much for Lady Cunard, and it caused a breach between mother and daughter which never healed.

Nancy's interest in Negroes was not confined to Henry Crowder alone. The whole Negro cause became an obsession with her. In 1935 she privately printed a vast anthology called *Negro* which she hoped would 'support the communist party's claim to be the champion of the black race worldwide'. Unfortunately for her aspirations, the book was too much like a tract and too bulky to be a popular success. Not until it was re-issued in a slimmer form in 1970 did it receive serious

attention, and even that was tempered by its curiosity value.

To be rich, comparatively young and possessed of even a minor talent in Paris in the 1920s was to live in Arcady. The exchange rate favoured foreigners and the French had all the advantages of liberalization without the disadvantage of having to sacrifice artistic freedom in its cause. Major talent, coupled with good looks and ambition, was invincible. Gabrielle Chanel, whose rise from seamstress to dress designer and friend of the great was meteoric even by French standards, was the personification of such social and artistic mobility. Her fluid, simple clothes were equally at home on the backs of the 'blasé society of women hankering after emancipation, tomboys with long cigarette holders and ambiguous, even perverse attitudes' as they were in Poulenc's parody of the same women in *Les Biches*. She dressed the golf player, one of the passengers in Cocteau's *Le Train Bleu*, in an outfit that bore a strong resemblance to one of those worn by the Prince of Wales while playing golf at le Touquet: 'a white collar, tightly knotted tie, and along with his plus-fours, a striped sweater with matching socks.' The Duke of Westminster, an acquaintance of the Prince's, and rather more than an acquaintance of Chanel's (his daily appearances at the rehearsals in the Theatre des Champs Elysées gave rise to much speculation) remarked that it was 'perfectly smart'.

All Chanel's charms, and they were considerable, could not turn her admirer into a husband, however much she might long to be a Duchess. When it came to the crunch the Duke wanted an heir and at forty-six Chanel was unlikely to be able to provide him with one. Two years later she retired gracefully from the race and the Duke married Loelia Ponsonby.

During a visit to Paris by the Duke and his new bride they stayed at the Hotel Lotti. As usual the staff were anxious to please and when the Duke, late one night, rang the bell and asked for a peach, it was soon sent up to him. Neither the Duke nor the Duchess thought very much of this at the time, and would never have thought of it again had not a strange man approached the Duchess at a party some years later. He told her he remembered her and her husband well, as he had once been a waiter in the Hotel Lotti. Furthermore it had been he who, on pain of instant dismissal, had been sent out to find a peach for Bendor the night he had rung for one, as there was none in the hotel. He had little hope of success, as all the shops were shut so, as the Duchess said in her memoirs:

. . . he wandered forlornly about until he saw a small greengrocer's with a basket of peaches in the window. Desperately he rattled the door, pounded on it, but all in vain. He dared not go back empty-handed so, as the street was quite deserted, he picked up a cobblestone from a heap where the road was being mended, smashed the window, seized a peach and dashed back to the Lotti, happy to think he had kept his job.

The Duke could not be expected to know or care how his whims were gratified, for the pleasures of the rich are usually at the expense of the poor. Nor could he possibly know that shortly afterwards the waiter left the Lotti of his own accord and achieved international recognition as a writer under the pseudonym George Orwell.

Below left: Iris Tree was one of the initial eight contributors to Nancy Cunard's Hours Press, established in Paris.

Below: Gabrielle Chanel opened her first fashion house in Paris in 1924. She revolutionized women's clothes, introducing a note of simplicity and comfort.

The Woman I Love

On 17 January 1936 King George V, from long force of habit, made an entry in his diary, 'I feel rotten.' Three days later, propped up in a four-poster bed in his red-carpetted bedroom at Sandringham House and surrounded by the Queen and all his children, except the Duke of Gloucester, who was himself ill, he lay near to death. Lord Dawson of Penn, the Royal Physician, and Sir Maurice Cassidy, a heart specialist, administered oxygen and heart massage in an attempt to stave off the debilitating attack of bronchial catarrh from which the King had been suffering for several months. Outside the Sandringham estate reporters and photographers waited in mournful anticipation for news of the King's progress.

At twenty five past nine in the morning of 20 January it was announced that, 'The King's life is moving peacefully to its close', and at five to twelve that night he died. As her biographer James Pope-Hennessy wrote, Queen Mary instantly:

in a gesture of historic impart, took the hand of her eldest son in hers and, stooping, kissed it. The King who had been Queen Mary's husband was dead. The King who was her son lived on – His most Excellent Majesty Edward the Eighth, by the Grace of God, of Great Britain, Ireland, and the British Dominions beyond the Seas, King, Defender of the Faith, Emperor of India.

Previous page: An unusual portrait of the Duchess of Windsor, taken by society photographer, Cecil Beaton.

Below: Newspaper placards in Fleet Street at 11.00 pm on 20 January 1936. King George V died at 11.55 pm that night.

As soon as his mother acknowledged him as the new King, Edward VIII broke down. The Archbishop of Canterbury, Dr Lang, noticed that all the sons, and especially the Prince of Wales, were 'painfully upset' but put it down to the fact that none of them had seen death before. A lady-in-waiting was also struck by the intensity of the Prince's grief and, no doubt remembering the distantly polite relationship he had had with his father during his lifetime, thought it 'frantic and unreasonable'.

After a bit, however, the King composed himself and left the room. He went to the telephone and asked to be connected to Mrs Wallis Simpson in London. According to the Duchess of Windsor, who had every reason to remember the incident, he said, 'It's all over, darling! Papa died a few moments ago.' She was the first person apart from those who had witnessed it to know of King George's death.

Queen Mary, had she known, would not have approved at all. She already knew of the existence of Mrs Simpson, who had been presented at Court on 10 June 1931, but had not allowed herself to dwell on the extent of her son's involvement with her. Such matters were not, in any case, easy to discuss. Natural diffidence forbade her to probe too deeply into the Prince's private life and extreme reserve and fear of her husband's abrasive

Above: King George V lies in State in Westminster Hall. He died on 20 January 1936.

Left: Edward, the Prince of Wales, in flying kit in 1932 during the inspection of the HMS *Courageous* with the Home Fleet.

Above: St James's Palace, 1923. The Prince of Wales spent much of his time in his own apartments here rather than with his parents in Buckingham Palace.

Far right: The beautiful Morgan sisters, Thelma and Gloria. Thelma enjoyed the Prince's attentions after her marriage to Lord Furness.

Below: The Prince of Wales met Freda Dudley Ward by chance, and was passionately in love with her for ten years.

temper inhibited discussion of the matter with him. The very idea of the King having a heart to heart with his son on the subject was unthinkable. He might criticize his clothes, or complain about his cockney accent, but to confront him with a specific incidence of undesirable behaviour, or to speak openly of an unsuitable liaison, would have been out of the question.

Part of the difficulty lay with the prince himself. He had resisted strongly all attempts to find him a suitable bride, an attitude which had saddened and worried his parents. It was not only the fact that the succession to the throne was not assured; they both believed strongly that the state of marriage offered 'certainly the safest and possibly the happiest solution to the problem of human life' and that without such a blessing life was a lonely and difficult affair.

Neither the King or the Queen had hide-bound rules about who their children should marry – gone were the days when only the sons and daughters of princes of the blood would do. They had tacitly agreed that if any of them were to choose from the English nobility they would not stand in their way. Two of them had already done so, Princess Mary having married Lord Lascelles and the Duke of York Lady Elizabeth Bowes-Lyon.

Unfortunately for his mother, who hoped that it might inspire him to do likewise, the Prince of Wales continued to amuse himself as a bachelor. Even more unfortunately, he

found dining *en famille* at Buckingham Palace dull and he began to spend more and more time away from home in his own apartments in St James's Palace. There he asserted himself by dressing his footmen in black (instead of royal scarlet), going out at night in a dinner jacket (instead of the regulation tails and white tie demanded of an officer in the Welsh Guards), smoking cigarettes and mixing himself cocktails. The King boiled over with frustrated irritation: 'You have had a much freer life than I ever knew, but don't think this means that you can now act like other people. Never forget your position and who you are.' The Queen, although she admired the impact her son made wherever he went, could not help wishing that he would not be quite so democratic. She herself was obsessively devoted to the idea of royalty as a race apart – the result of having been born the child of a morganatic marriage and having been dismissed as not *ebenbürtig* (correctly born) by other German princelings. If her son would not marry a royal princess (and she had to admit that most of them were German and therefore offensive to the British) the very least he could do was to maintain a dignified standard of behaviour. Even if he would not do as his father wished, he could at least obey the orders of his monarch.

The Prince of Wales had no intention of modifying his pleasures to suit his parents, feeling that he had a right to a life of his own. He had, after all, asserted his independence in more satisfactory ways. During the First World War he had insisted on taking a commission in the Grenadier Guards and on spending time in the field with the Allied armies. He had been awarded the Military Cross and the *Croix de Guerre*. After the war his series of world tours to promote British trade had been a triumph. From Buenos Aires to Mandalay he had been acclaimed as a conquering hero. 'Wherever this "prince of princes" went', wrote one correspondent, 'his smile, modesty, fearlessness and boyish good looks won every heart, and orders and commissions blossomed in his footprints.'

He had also fallen in love. While on leave from the front in 1918 he had met Mrs Freda Dudley Ward, then married to William Dudley Ward, who was both the Liberal Member of Parliament for Southampton and Vice-Chamberlain of the Royal Household. They met by chance. Freda had been to a dinner party without her husband and was being escorted home by Buster Dominguez, a young Latin-American diplomat. On their way across Belgrave Square warning signals announced a Zeppelin air-raid. They sheltered in the doorway of No 31. After a bit, according J Brian III and Charles J V Murphy, biographers of the Duke and Duchess of

Windsor, 'a torrent of young people in evening dress uniform poured down the staircase, led by the hostess. She saw the couple and went towards them.' Reassured by their respectable appearance, she invited them into the basement with the rest of the party. There 'in the semi-gloom, a young man attached himself to Freda and began chatting.' When the all-clear sounded she made a move to leave, but her companion would not hear of it and the hostess, too, tried to detain her: '. . . do come upstairs. His Royal Highness is so anxious for you to do so.' Thus persuaded, Mrs Dudley Ward went to the ball. The Prince danced with her until three o'clock, when the music stopped. He then took her home and 'begged to come in just for a minute', but Freda refused, on the grounds that she was staying with her mother-in-law.

For the next ten years the Prince remained, in Frances Donaldson's words, 'passionately and abjectly' in love with her. He telephoned every morning, and, after she had moved into a house of her own in St John's Wood, called to see her every afternoon at five o'clock. Official engagements permitting, he accompanied her everywhere – to private parties, to

nightclubs, to the Cavendish Hotel and to the races. Her two daughters adopted him as a surrogate father, nicknaming him 'the little Prince'. When he was away he left the only other objects of his devotion, his two Cairn terriers, for her to look after.

He relied on her utterly and told her all his troubles. She, for her part, was perfectly discreet and endlessly obliging, but also outspoken. Tales of the humiliations he had to suffer at the hands of his parents met with a brisk response. 'I tried to put some stuffing into him', she said, 'I told him, "you don't *have* to take any more! Stand up for yourself!"' Complaints of the burdens he had to bear as heir to the throne and his longing to have a life of his own 'like ordinary people' were also summarily dealt with. She told him firmly what he already knew – that it was impossible: 'he was not an ordinary person, but born to be a King, and there was no escaping it.'

This idyll might have lasted for ever, had it not been for Thelma Furness. Born Thelma Morgan, she, her twin sister Gloria, and her elder sister Consuela were the daughters of an American father and a Spanish mother. All were beautiful. Beaton described the twins in his *Book of Beauty* as being, 'alike as two magnolias . . . With their marble complexions, raven tresses and flowing dresses . . .with their slight lisps and foreign accents . . . [they diffused] an Onida atmosphere of hothouse elegance and lacy feminity . . .' All married well; Gloria married Reggie Vander-

bilt, Consuelo an up-and-coming diplomat called Benjamin Thaw and Thelma, after a shaky start with a man twice her age, settled for Lord 'Duke' Furness, an extremely rich middle-aged peer with red hair and an unpredictable temperament.

To her chagrin, Thelma soon found that once the novelty of having a young bride (she was twenty one) had worn off, her husband returned to his former pursuits – hunting, which she disliked, gambling, which he preferred to do alone, and the company of other women. She was left by herself in Leicestershire to look after their son and to muse over what had gone wrong with their marriage.

Given Thelma's lively nature it was unlikely that she would have languished for long in solitary confinement. It came as a welcome diversion when the prince of Wales came to Leicestershire in 1929 in order to hand out rosettes for the prize-winning cows at the Annual Fair and, when he had finished, turned his attention to her. '[He] seemed to me to be winsomely handsome', she wrote afterwards, '. . . the quintessence of charm. And after the swaggering earthiness of Duke, his shyness and reserve had a distinct appeal.' The Prince managed to overcome his shyness for long enough to ask Lady Furness to dine with him at St James's Palace, an invitation she accepted with alacrity.

From then on Mrs Dudley Ward saw rather less of him, although he continued to rely on her for advice and support. In particular he was anxious for her help in refurbishing a country house he had just acquired, a castellated eighteenth-century Gothic folly in Windsor Great Park called Fort Belvedere. Previously occupied by an old friend of the King's, it had fallen into a state of total disrepair and when the Prince asked his father if he could have it, he was amazed: 'What could you possibly want that old place for? Those damned weekends, I suppose . . . Well, if you want it, it's yours.'

In a transport of proprietorial enthusiasm the Prince threw himself into putting his new acquisition to rights. Every minute he could spare from his official duties was spent motoring down to Windsor to see how the improvements that he and Mrs Dudley Ward had planned were getting on. Canalettos were hung in the drawing room and Stubbs in the dining room, furniture was begged and borrowed from Windsor Castle and Freda agonized over colours, wallpapers and chair covers.

The Prince developed a latent interest in horticulture. He spent long hours hacking away at the undergrowth in the weed-infested garden. On an official visit to the Chelsea Flower Show a rockery caught his eye. At once he ordered it to be sent, lock stock and barrel, down to the Fort. The delighted gardeners lugged the whole thing down to Windsor Great Park and found the Prince, in deceptively casual clothes, waiting for them. 'I want those rocks moved *here* he told the workmen, pointing to a spot ten feet from where the expert had placed them, 'and I want the foxgloves and Canterbury Bells over *there*. . . .' In vain they tried to tell him that that was not the way it was at Chelsea. They might just as well have given up there and then. The Prince had visualized how it would be in his garden and no amount of pleading on the part of the wounded landscape gardeners would make him change his mind. As Sir John Aired, his equerry, remarked:

The result was, the pattern, so carefully designed for the connoisseurs at the flower show, was knocked hopelessly awry. The expert flung off, speechless with indignation. His workmen followed. H.R.H. quickly lost interest, and when I last saw the rock garden some years later, it was still unfinished.

As soon as the Fort was habitable, the Prince installed himself there every weekend. But it was not Freda Dudley Ward but Thelma Furness who presided over these weekend parties, an indignity which Freda suffered in silence. Thelma, on the other hand, although flattered by the Prince's attentions, found herself hostess to a rather different *ménage* than the one she had expected. Weekends at the Fort were very far from bacchanalian.

Exactly what Lady Furness hoped to gain

from her friendship with royalty is not known, but given her proclivity for night life, it is a matter for surprise that she settled for such a quiet time. The fact was, the Prince had a domestic streak. He liked nothing better than a good stint in the garden, followed by a hearty tea and, much later (about half past eight) to make up his own cocktails for his guests, followed by a simple meal of grilled or roast meat, salads, a souffle and cheese, washed down by some light wine and, after dinner, to dance a quickstep to the gramaphone. Early to bed and early to rise was his nursery motto and he stuck to it until death. Thelma, pushing all thoughts of London night life firmly to the back of her mind, went along with this regime with complete docility. Knowing his fondness for lively pretty young women, she took it upon herself to invite some of her friends to the Fort. One of them was a friend of her sister Consuelo's called Wallis Simpson.

The story of Wallis Simpson's introduction to the Prince of Wales has been well documented, as has her early life. She was born in 1896, the daughter of an impeccably-bred Maryland family. Her widowed mother was a

Above: Mrs Wallis Simpson photographed during her short-lived marriage to Lieutenant Win Spencer.

Right: Mrs Simpson, the woman who roused a king and a nation.

Below: Ernest Simpson, Wallis's second husband.

Montague from Virginia whose parents had supported the Confederate cause during the Civil War and her grandmother nursed such an abiding hatred of Northerners that she never allowed one over her threshold. She was brought up frugally, she was good at games and lessons, she made her debut at a Baltimore ball in December 1914 and in November 1916, partly for love and partly to relieve her mother of the burden of supporting her, she married Lieutenant Win Spencer, a naval aviator.

Shortly afterwards it became apparent that the marriage was a mistake. Win had a restless and melancholy nature and to brighten things up drank heavily, and Wallis turned to her family for advice on how to go about getting a divorce. She did not meet with a sympathetic response. No Warfield or Montague had ever been party to such a thing. It was tantamount to blasphemy. Wallis was told in no uncertain terms to make every attempt to reconcile herself to her husband and if all else failed to separate as quietly and discreetly as possible. Divorce was out of the question.

Wallis, however, would not listen to

reason. If her family would not help her she must help herself. She discovered that she could obtain an easy and cheap divorce for desertion by living in the state of Virginia for one year. She therefore lodged in an hotel in Warrenton and prepared to lead a life of solitary virtue, her only company a pile of good, improving books.

These admirable aims were soon undermined. There was the irresistible temptation of dinners and parties with Virginia's horsey set. There was the equally irresistible prospect of trips to New York. It was on a visit to her old friend Mary Raffray's house in Washington Square that she met Ernest Simpson. They found they had a great deal in common. He, too, was waiting for a divorce. He, too, was a voracious reader and he lent her books to take Warrenton. They got along famously.

Ernest Simpson has always been a rather shadowy figure in the development of the Windsor story. Photographs show him to be a bluff and genial figure, well groomed and prosperous looking. English by birth – his father was head of a firm of shipbrokers, Simpson, Spence and Young, which had offices in London and New York – his American mother saw to it that he was brought up and educated in New York. In 1918, in his third year at Harvard, he left to enlist in the Officer Cadet Battalion of the Household Brigade and was later gazetted Second Lieutenant in the Coldstream Guards, but never saw

active service. He did, however, win the right to wear the Guards tie and blazer, a privilege he much enjoyed. He also sported a small moustache and a bowler hat and acquired an English accent, much to the amazement of his old Harvard friends who remembered him in more nondescript apparel.

What particular attraction he held for Wallis is wrapped in mystery. Possibly his dogged determination to marry her had something to do with it; also the fact that she was running short of money and had tried and failed to forge a career for herself in the fashion world. Whatever the reason, as soon as both of them were free to do so they married. The wedding ceremony took place on 21 July 1928 in London, where Ernest had gone to take over his father's business, and the honeymoon was spent motoring round Europe in a yellow Lagonda.

On their return they took a house in Upper Berkeley Street, and Wallis devoted herself to housekeeping and penetrating the mysteries of English social life. The second she found more difficult than the first. She had always been a talented housekeeper, was an excellent cook and had managed very well on Win's naval salary. They had been renowned for the delicious French food she had conjured up and for the elegant informality of their parties. Wallis looked forward keenly to enjoying the same sort of success as Ernest's wife. London, however, was not Atlanta and England was not America. Although Ernest's sister, Mrs Kerr-Smiley (who had given the party in Belgrave Square ten years before at which Mrs Dudley Ward had met the Prince of Wales) introduced the new Mrs Simpson to her friends, Wallis at first found her new acquaintances reserved and cold. She missed the spontaneous American habit of picking up the telephone to invite people round on the spur of the moment and shuddered at the chilly English custom of issuing printed invitations weeks in advance.

Eventually she managed to compromise and succeeded in establishing a style and a circle of her own. They bought the lease of a flat in Bryanston Court, which Wallis decorated to her own taste: pale-green walls and cream damask curtains for the drawing room, a glass-topped table, white leather chairs and white wallpaper with rust-coloured figures for the dining room. Every day she was at

home at six o'clock, and those who dropped in to what Chips Channon described cattily as 'that dreadful, banal flat', found their hostess mixing outlandish cocktails in small shakers and casting a professional eye on the plates of succulent canapés she had prepared for them to eat. The abundance of stiff drinks, the enticing food and the unflagging high spirits of Wallis made Bryanston Court popular with an ever-growing bevy of hungry and thirsty actors, diplomats, ambassadors, journalists and members of parliament, all of whom found a visit there cheaper and more entertaining than their clubs.

Full recognition of the Simpson's capacity for making friends and influencing people came when Consuelo Thaw asked them to stand in for her as chaperone for her sister Thelma Furness, who was entertaining the Prince of Wales for the weekend at her hunting lodge, Burrough Court, in Leicestershire. Ernest was beside himself with pride and joy at such an honour but Wallis, although she was naturally curious to meet the Prince, at first demurred. She would not know how to behave in such exalted company. She did not

All pictures: Although Edward chose Mrs Simpson rather than the Crown, he enjoyed much popular support and his abdication saddened his people.

Right: Edward and Wallis on their wedding day, 3 June 1937. They were married in France. After his abdication he was given the title Duke of Windsor.

Left: The news of Edward's abdication was a shock to the general public, who had heard little of his association with Mrs Simpson.

Below left: The official proclamation of George VI's accession to the throne.

WHEREAS by an Instrument of Abdication dated the Tenth day of December instant His former Majesty King *Edward* the Eighth did declare His irrevocable Determination to renounce the Throne for Himself and His Descendants, and the said Instrument of Abdication has now taken effect, whereby the Imperial Crown of *Great Britain, Ireland* and all other His former Majesty's dominions is now solely and rightfully come to the High and Mighty Prince *Albert Frederick Arthur George*: We, therefore, the Lords Spiritual and Temporal of this Realm, being here assisted with these of His former Majesty's Privy Council, with Numbers of other Principal Gentlemen of Quality, with the Lord Mayor, Aldermen, and Citizens of *London*, do now hereby with one Voice and Consent of Tongue and Heart, publish and proclaim, That the High and Mighty Prince *Albert Frederick Arthur George* is now become our only lawful and rightful Liege Lord *George* the Sixth by the Grace of God, of *Great Britain, Ireland* and the *British Dominions* beyond the Seas King, Defender of the Faith, Emperor of *India* : To whom we do acknowledge all Faith and constant Obedience, with all hearty and humble Affection: beseeching God, by whom Kings and Queens do reign, to bless the Royal Prince *George* the Sixth with long and happy Years to reign over us.

Given at *St. James's Palace,* this Twelfth day of *December* in the year of our Lord One thousand nine hundred and thirty-six.

GOD SAVE THE KING

know how to curtsey. She knew nothing about hunting and she had a cold coming on. Consuelo brushed all these objections aside as being too ridiculous for words. Of course she could manage; her husband Benjamin, would escort them to Burrough Court and look after them in every way. There was nothing to worry about at all.

The Simpsons travelled by train to Melton Mowbray with Mr Thaw, who at Wallis's insistence, showed her how to curtsey. 'Together' wrote Lady Moseley, 'they wobbled on the floor of the railway carriage.' The weekend itself went off better than they had dared hope. Despite her cold Wallis managed to keep up a flow of bright and informed conversation and despite her nerves managed to keep the prince entertained when she found herself seated next to him at lunch. Although she was too agitated to remember what they said to each other, the Prince's looks made a deep impression on her: '. . . the slightly wind-rumpled hair, the turned-up nose, and a strange, wistful almost sad look about the eyes when his expression was in repose.' She, like others before her, responded to his little-boy-lost look. As Freda Dudley Ward put it, 'Every woman who saw that sad little face felt she had just the shoulder for him to cry on.'

Soon after the house party broke up the Prince went off on one of his trips abroad. Four months later, in April 1931, to celebrate his return, Thelma gave an afternoon reception and the Simpsons were invited. In June Wallis was presented at Court, and it was then that the Prince singled her out for special attention. He was, he said, 'struck by the grace and dignity of her movements'. Later, at a champagne party given by Thelma, he com-

Foreign Comment

QUEENLY ENIGMA: What Will Mrs. Simpson and King Edward Do? Asks Wondering World

Nobody mentioned the King. For that matter, no British newspaper mentioned that Mrs. Simpson was his friend.

But minutes before the Baltimore belle slipped out of Ipswich Assizes with her second divorce in her pocket, a million conversations were being launched around the world with the phrase:

"Now that she's free—"

Javanese and New Yorkers and Icelanders wondered, whether, "now that she's free," the American woman would:

1. Fade out of the picture as Wallis Warfield to spare her "Davey" any embarrassment;

2. Simply continue to be Mrs. Simpson, "his closest friend";

3. Become his morganatic wife;

4. Become his Queen Consort, his inferior and subject, thereby enjoying the following ancient prerogatives:

a. The making of grants, gifts, or contracts without the King;

b. Suing and being sued without the King;

c. Receiving by gift from her husband;

d. Having her courts and offices as if she were a sole person;

e. Holding for treason those who plot against her life;

f. Being tried by her own equals for offenses;

g. Receiving her ancient revenue of Queen Gold (personal revenue).

There is no law to prevent the King's making her his Queen, if he wishes. Even the established Church of England could perform the ceremony, for under the Divorce Laws of 1857, divorced people may remarry in church. A prelate or clergyman need not officiate if he objects, but he may not refuse the use of his church, or forbid another clergyman to officiate.

Inconsistency—In practise, the Church's attitude is contradictory: while refusing to admit there is such a thing as divorce, it takes a stand against it. Four years ago the Archbishop of Canterbury, Primate of All England, close friend of the Queen Mother, and traditional officiating clergyman at a royal marriage ceremony, voiced his "desire that in the case of any person previously married, who has been separated by divorce from a husband or wife who is still alive, the marriage should not be solemnized in church."

Socially, too, British royalty frowns on divorce. Queen Mary refused to receive divorcées in court, following the example of her strong-willed mother-in-law, Queen Victoria, devoting her life to Prince Albert's sainted memory, also even frowned on the remarriage of widows, altho she was the child of a widow's second union.

But times are changing under the new King, tradition after tradition is being shattered.

Whereas Parliament could not forbid the match, it could ban "Queen Wally's" children from the throne. Moreover, it could cut or abolish the King's public income of $2,700,000 a year. At present, he does not receive $600,000 of this amount—

As her friends see "Wallis": an intimate sketch made by a friend of Mrs Wallis Simpson last summer while she and the King were vacationing in Vienna

Second marriage: the certificate issued at London's General Register Office in 1928 to Mrs. Wallis Warfield Spencer and Mr. Ernest Aldrich Simpson

Above: The Literary Digest wonders how Edward and Mrs Simpson will resolve the problem of the King being involved with a twice-divorced woman, 7 November 1936.

Right: A rare shot of the Duke and Duchess of Windsor on their honeymoon cruise. The couple were spotted by a photographer on the Dalmatian coast.

Far right: An official photograph of the couple on honeymoon in the grounds of Castle Wasserleonburg.

plimented Wallis on her appearance and when the Simpsons rose to leave he asked if he could give them a lift home. The astonished and rapturous Ernest, whose worship of royalty verged on the insane, agreed with alacrity. Blinded by excitement he did not see the danger signals; and by the time he did it was too late.

Bit by bit the bonds were formed. There were invitations to Fort Belvedere. The Prince took to dropping in at Bryanston Court on his way to St John's Wood for a chat and a drink, but more and more often he forgot about St John's Wood and stayed on to dinner. He found Wallis extraordinarily pleasant company. Apart from her looks, which he much admired, and her clothes, which were always immaculate, she took a genuine interest in his work—the only woman, as he told her, who had ever done so. He admired her efficiency and her attention to detail, and he loved her wisecracks and her gaiety. Susceptible as ever, the Prince fell in love. But this time the object of his affections was a woman who

cloaked her iron fist in a velvet glove. Hunting the fox might not be her forte but stalking the English had proved a worthy substitute. Now that she had cornered the richest prize in their jewelled crown, who was she to let it go?

As for Lady Furness and Mrs Dudley Ward, they both, in different ways, miscalculated the situation. In 1934 Thelma went to America to visit her sister Gloria and, seeing that Wallis and the Prince were getting on so well, asked her to keep an eye on him for her while she was away. She returned, in a blaze of publicity and surrounded by rumours of a shipboard romance with Aly Khan, to find Wallis ensconced at the Fort and the Prince distant and annoyed at her seemingly inconstant behaviour. She noticed that Wallis and the Prince appeared to have an endless fund of private jokes. When at dinner one night Wallis playfully smacked the Prince's hand, an unheard-of breach of etiquette, for eating a bit of lettuce with his fingers, Thelma at last realized what had happened in her absence. She met Wallis's eyes and they were steely and predatory. 'That one cold, defiant glance' told her everything, and next day she packed her bags and left.

Mrs Dudley Ward, on the other hand, had no idea of the way things were at all. She knew of Thelma's existence and had resigned herself to sharing the Prince with her, but of Mrs Simpson she knew little or nothing. One morning in May 1934, after an interval of a few days spent nursing one of her daughters, she telephoned St James's Palace to tell the Prince that things were now back to normal. The telephonist, who had connected her for the past sixteen years, could hardly bring

himself to tell her that he had orders not to put her through. She never heard from the Prince of Wales again.

It was not only Lady Furness and Mrs Dudley Ward who miscalculated the situation. Although it soon became obvious to even the dullest witted that the Prince had a new favourite, it was assumed by the majority that it would be as transitory an attachment as the others. Nevertheless, ever eager to be at the centre of things, Lady Cunard and Lady Colefax vied with each other to catch this rising star in the ascendant. Wallis found herself besieged with invitations to lunch, to dinner, to cocktails. Chips Channon, another expatriate American, whose rise up the social ladder had been every bit as meteoric, watched her progress with grudging admiration. On 23 January 1935, after meeting her at lunch at Lady Cunard's, he recorded in his diary that she seemed, 'a nice quiet, well-bred mouse of a woman . . . I think she is rather surprised and rather conscience-stricken by her present position and the limelight which consequently falls upon her.' Several months later they met again, in Emerald Cunard's box at the opera. He noted the 'extraordinary hold Mrs Simpson has over the prince' and watched with horrified fascination as, 'she made him take a cigar from his breast pocket. "It doesn't look very pretty", she said.'

Ernest, meanwhile, had had his devotion to royalty stretched to the uttermost. He confided in Wallis's aunt, revealing his divided loyalties and his fears for his disintegrating marriage: 'I'm a British subject and it's an honour for me to have the Prince sit at my table and accept us as his friends', but 'This thing has hit us like an avalanche. Wallis can't seem to stop it'. Sadly for Ernest, the prince sat less and less at his table. He was too busy taking Wallis out to supper, or arranging parties to go to Vienna, on cruises in the Mediterranean, or for summer holidays in Cannes. He invited Ernest, but somehow these trips always seemed to come at times when he had to be away on business. On one of these visits to New York 'sometime in 1935', he looked up his old friend Mary Raffray, whom Wallis had urged to keep an eye on him. With a symmetry not often found in real life, Mrs Raffray, like Wallis for Thelma Furness, did her job rather too well. Ernest fell in love and, most conveniently, slipped out of sight. The roundelay was almost complete.

Not quite, however. Dark rumours that the Prince's latest obsession might be more serious than had first been supposed had filtered through to Lambeth Palace. Soon after the accession, therefore, the Archbishop of Canterbury, Dr Cosmo Lang, sought an audience with his new King – a prospect neither rel-

Above: Edward and Wallis pose for photographers in the grounds of their new residence in France, 1937.

Left: The Duchess of Windsor was photographed by Cecil Beaton for *Vogue* magazine in 1937.

hole-in-the-corner romance, he had resolved to bring it out into the open. It was all too simple – Wallis must divorce Ernest, they must marry, and she must be crowned Queen and Empress of India at his side. Nothing else would do, nothing else was good enough for the woman he loved.

The complexities of such acts appeared to have eluded both of them. The King, while realizing that the situation posed certain ecclesiastical and constitutional difficulties, was naively confident that his will could overcome what seemed to him to be manageable laws. Wallis, who was not renowned for her grasp of English affairs, and who had a blind faith in the ultimate power of the King, also thought that his will could prevail. Neither of them was prepared to face up to the fact that, should the weight of the establishment be turned against them, they were doomed to ignominious failure and extinction. How could they not win, when their cause was just and equitable? When it came to the test who would deny them their love?

Unfortunately for them, star-crossed lovers were not part of Anglo-Saxon romantic heritage. Celts, yes, even the Scots, but an English King and an American upstart divorcee, definitely no. Stanley Baldwin, whose unenviable job it was as Prime Minister to warn the King that the English people would not stand for his proposed marriage, had at least that on his side. Nothing, not even his overwhelming popularity, could overcome obstacles of such magnitude. They could not be overcome, they could not even be contemplated. He told the King in no uncertain terms that he must either give up Mrs Simpson or abdicate. If he did not, the cabinet would resign and the King would be in the unhappy position of being unable to call upon a single alternative Prime Minister to serve him.

Confused and browbeaten by these threats the King fled to Fort Belvedere to rally his wits. Whenever he could get away he drove to London to talk things over with Wallis, who waited impatiently for his visits at her new house in Cumberland Terrace. During the past months she had acquired a taste for royal privileges – the jewels, the formalities waived, the protection and the adulation – and needed reassurance that they would not suddenly be snatched from her grasp. But however much the King might delude himself, by including Wallis in the Court Circular, by transporting her on a magic carpet to Yugoslavia and Greece in the luxurious yacht *Nahlin*, or by imagining that she could slip away to Ipswich and obtain a decree unnoticed by the world press, it was becoming apparent even to him that it could not last much longer.

On 27 October 1936 Wallis was granted her divorce amid a blaze of publicity. Mr

ished. The relationship between the Archbishop and Edward VIII had never been an easy one. As Prince of Wales he had been a poor churchgoer, confining his attendance to weddings, funerals, christenings, state occasions and the odd visit to St Geroge's Chapel for evensong. He had, as his biographers pointed out, lamentably 'failed to show even perfunctory curiosity about either the troubled affairs of the State faith, of which he was now the sworn defender, or the problems of the large ecclesiastical establishment of which he was the principal ornament and titular authority.'

If that was not bad enough, there was now the distasteful matter of his sovereign's involvement with a twice-married woman to be broached, for it would be unthinkable for Dr Lang to administer communion at the Coronation to a monarch who was patently sinning in word and deed against the precepts of his Church. Not surprisingly, the interview did not go well. The King was on edge and the Archbishop did not help matters by persistent references to 'your conduct'. They parted on terms of mutual distrust.

Had be but known it, the Archbishop had good reason for suspicion. By that time, the King was more deeply involved than he, or anyone else, knew. Not satisfied with his

Baldwin, who had a dogged streak and in any case was becoming heartily sick of the whole business (he never had much time for the King and made no secret of the fact that he thought the Duke of York would do the job a great deal better) pursued him to the Fort and continued to press for a decision. Backed into a corner the King tried one last trick. Would it not be possible for Mrs Smpson to become his wife and not his Queen – a morganatic marriage? Mr Baldwin hummed and hawed and went away and consulted the Dominions. The answer was no. They were uniformly against the idea.

On 1 December an obscure bishop who knew nothing of Mrs Simpson remarked during the course of an address to a diocesan conference, that 'the King was in urgent need of God's grace'. He was alluding to the forthcoming coronation, but as far as the long-suffering British press was concerned it was enough to open the floodgates. So far the press had restrained themselves with uncharacteristic decency but the next day every newspaper in the country carried pictures of the King and Mrs Simpson and banner headlines announced 'Abdication'. Horrified, Wallis fled the country to France and the King was left on his own to cope with the situation as best he could. He was supported by Lord Rothermere and Lord Beaverbrook, each of whom for reasons of his own supported the morganatic marriage and who attempted to form a 'King's Party' to aid their cause. The King was harassed by his mother, Queen Mary, whose straightbacked adherence to duty, particularly when it was a royal one, was unflinching. Consumed by fear of the consequences of upsetting the constitution, Edward VIII finally came to a decision. He could go on no longer, he was both incapable of and temperamentally unsuited to such a struggle. On 11 December 1936 he spoke, at last, to his people. He told them of his love, of his conflict, of his loyalty to his brother, the new King, and of his intention to 'quit altogether public affairs'. His people listened in silence. 'The whole of the English-speaking world' wrote an American commentator, 'all but stood still for seventy seconds. People wept. There had never been its match for pathos: a King – a King of England! renouncing his imperial splendour for love alone . . . it was the greatest news story since the Resurrection.'

As for the English, they might well have speculated how this Prince, who seemed to have found the elixir of youth, whose popularity had turned his journeys into the depressed areas of his kingdom into triumphal marches, and who could be forgiven anything, even a morganatic and distasteful marriage, had come to this.

Left: After their marriage, the Duke and Duchess of Windsor lived in voluntary exile in France.

The New Politics

While the American press was drowning in a sea of sickly prose, the more restrained end of the British magazine market kept a stiff upper lip. On 17 December the *Queen* produced its regular fortnightly issue. The cover displayed a picture of the new King and Queen, with the caption 'God Bless their Majesties'. There was no mention of the abdication and, apart from an oblique reference to the fact that Queen Elizabeth was of British descent, none of Mrs Simpson. Instead, readers were urged to extend their 'affectionate and heartfelt good wishes' to King George VI and his consort, who now stood as the 'embodiment of this realm and its centuries of great tradition', and were invited to speculate about arrangements for the forthcoming Coronation. It was as though, as Quentin Crewe remarked, 'there had been no change in the *dramatis personae*'.

Such an attitude reminded the *Queen*'s readers, if they needed reminding, that the abdication was essentially an English affair, and had been dealt with in an English way. It did no good to rant and rave and there was little point in submitting to long bouts of painful self-examination. What was done was done and could not be undone. The establishment had closed ranks against the outsider that had threatened to corrupt its most hallowed member. Edward, bloody but unbowed, had been punished with that most awful of penalties for an Englishman – he had been obliged to cross the channel and become a foreigner.

In the aftermath of the abdication, those who had supported the ex-King ran for cover and waited for the hubbub to subside before emerging. Lady Cunard and Lady Colefax retreated in disarray. Gone now were Emerald Cunard's dreams of Queen Wallis and herself as Mistress of Robes, and gone were the excitements of royal dinners at Argyll House, the curtseys and the heady atmosphere of intrigue. The rats, as Osbert Sitwell observed in his unpublished poem 'National Rat Week', bared their teeth and ran.

Lady Diana Cooper, on the other hand, managed with some aplomb to have the best of both worlds. Even though she and her husband had been frequent visitors to the Fort and had accompanied the King and Mrs Simpson on their summer cruise in 1936, she was soon on excellent terms with the new King and Queen, whom she described as 'spellbinding'. Duff, she later explained, without batting an eyelid, 'had for many years idolised Queen Elizabeth'.

Previous page: British fascists march in procession on May Day, 1938.

Below: Sir Oswald Mosley stood as the Labour candidate in the 1926 by-election.

There were other, more dubious, allies who were touched by the abdication, and they were ones that the ex-King, for all his outspoken sympathy with the land of his forefathers, did not acknowledge. It was one thing to admire the strength and power of the new Nazi party and its leaders and to compare it unfavourably with the shilly-shallying democracy of the Baldwin government or, as patron of the British Legion, to seek to 'stretch forth the hand of friendship' to German ex-servicemen in the interests of international understanding and peace, but it was quite another to support the activities of the British Union of Fascists.

The BUF, however, supported the ex-King. The party was led by the suave and charismatic Sir Oswald Mosley, whose political career began in 1918 when he was elected Conservative member for Harrow at the age of twenty one, but lurched to the other side of the House in 1924, when he joined the Labour Party. In 1930 Mosley veered into the New Party which was founded in a move to combat the Labour Party's unemployment policy, and finally came to rest outside the parliamentary system in 1932 when he allied himself with fascism. The BUF was embarrassingly royalist to a man.

In Edward VIII they had, as Robert Skidelsky remarked, 'fascism's ideal king, young, unconventional, anti-Establishment, who stood for friendship with Germany and action on unemployment.' Edward was also, as Chips Channon wrote, 'against too much slipshod democracy' and nursed irrational fears against Soviet Russia. He once told a young American journalist writing about the General Election of 1945 that 'if Labour wins you can tear up your piece because Russia will take over the country in a few days.' No wonder they believed, with their Leader, that the King should be allowed to marry whom he wished and that it was an act of 'flagrant dictatorship' on the part of the government to divert him from his chosen path and 'hustle him from the throne without consulting the People.' No wonder, when the unthinkable happened and their figurehead departed, the heart went out of the BUF's monarchism.

Their king might have gone over the water, but the members of the British Fascist movement were determined to stay put and save the Empire without recourse to war. It was a lonely fight. Gone were the halcyon days of 1934, when Lord Rothermere in the *Daily Mail* cried 'Hurrah for the Blackshirts', and Lady Houston in the Saturday Review extolled their virtues in rapturous editorials (even launching into verse) and establishment luminaries like Sir Basil Liddell Hart, Sir Charles Petrie, Lord Lloyd and Philip Magnus dines as guests at the January Club. The movement, no longer the white hope of the right wing of the Conservative Party, had shrunk, as Robert Skidelsky said, 'to its proper dimen-

Above: Mosley left the Labour Party in 1929 after serving as a Member of Parliament. He resigned and later founded the British Union of Fascists.

sions – that of an infant movement trying to establish itself in conditions of economic recovery against a hostile political culture.'

The infant had, however, a macabre and precocious steak. Like the Midwich Cuckoos it had an exaggerated opinion of its capabilities. Behind lay half-forgotten longings for a simpler, more primitive life, where man pitted his wits against the storms of fate and singlehandedly overcame them, and in front lay the need to slay the modern dragons of social and economic deprivation. In between, in the hinterland of the spirit, lay the desire for rational control and direction of human life by any justifiable means and beneath, in the dark corners of the soul, irrational prejudice fomented in a cauldron of hate and fear.

To begin with, Sir Oswald took some pains to conceal the more unpalatable aims of his movement from his followers, dressing up its aspirations in a welter of high-minded rhetoric. Addressing the thirty two founder members at Great George Street on 1 October 1932 he exhorted them to 'dedicate their lives to building in this country a movement of the modern age . . . [to] be prepared to sacrifice all, but to do so for no small and unworthy ends', urging them, like all good disciples, to be prepared to 'face abuse, misunderstanding, bitter animosity and possibly the ferocity of struggle and danger'. In return they should expect no other reward than the satisfaction of knowing they were 'fighting that a great land may live. . . .' The faithful responded with devotional ardour. It was not so much what he said as how he said it. 'His eyes flashed fire, dilated and contracted like a mesmerists' wrote his cousin James Lees Milne, who had a lowly position as canvasser and bottle washer in the New Party:

His voice rose and fell in hypnotic cadences. He was madly in love with his own words. . . . The posturing, the grimacing, the switching on and off of those gleaming teeth, and the overall swashbuckling, so purposeful and calculated, were more likely to appeal to Mayfair flappers than to sway indigent workers. . . .

Sir Oswald's heady brand of extremism did, indeed, appeal to many of his own class. The sight of 'one of us' preaching so vigorously from the pulpit of positive politics and the mixture of aristocrat, corsair and visionary combined in his 'lithe and catlike' figure did much to attract susceptible members of both sexes. Lady Cunard, Diana Guiness and her sister Unity Mitford, Cyril Joad, John Strachey (Lytton's nephew), Harold Nicholson, the Sitwells and Bernard Shaw all at some time fell under his spell. The euphoria he generated swept doubts and hesitations aside. The daydreams he propagated were the desires and infatuations of adolescence, the steamy throbbing urges of star-struck young men and women, to whom all things were possible, if only they knew how to go about them. In Mosley they found their pied piper, ready to take command, inflame their longings and make their dreams come true.

Harold Nicholson, although at forty five no adolescent, found himself caught up in the mounting tide of excitement that surrounded the formation of the New Party. Personally at a low ebb, having left the diplomatic service in 1929 in order to be able to spend more time with his wife, Victoria Sackville-West, and disillusioned with his work as a journalist on the *Evening Standard* and the *Daily Express* (an occupation he found degrading and aesthetically unsatisfactory) he found himself having, as he wrote in his diary in October, 1930, 'dreams of power and youth'.

These longings were satisfied the following year, when he decided to stand as a candidate for the new Party. It was a challenge he was unable to resist. Here at last was adventure and a possibility of escape from the 'dismal realities' of middle age. Here, too, was a lead-

Below: George Bernard Shaw, dramatist and man of letters, at one time fell under the spell of Mosley's heady brand of politics.

er of physical charm and intellectual ability preaching a gospel of muscular politics – exactly the sort of hero to appeal to Nicholson's homosexual cravings for hearty upper-class undergraduates. This penchant was given rein after the captain of the Oxford Rugby team, Peter Howard, was introduced into the Party, bringing many a beefy enthusiast in his wake. As Robert Skidelsky pointed out, it was:

not least of the ironies of the Party's development that it should have been this fastidious, well-connected *habitué* of London's intellectual, literary world, with his dreams of youth and glory, who brought Mosley into contact with precisely that "fascistic" element that was soon to alarm John Strachey. . .and to give Mosley the reputation of commandeering thugs to support his political programme.

For his part, Mosley appreciated his new disciple. Not only was he malleable he was also a link with Beaverbrook, whose co-operation would greatly improve the party's chances of success at the forthcoming General Election.

Above: Victoria Sackville-West at Long Barn Weals in 1924. She had married Harold Nicholson in 1913.

Left: In 1931 Harold Nicholson stood as a candidate for Mosley's newly formed party. Like the other 24 candidates, he was defeated.

Beaverbrook, however, was not as starry-eyed as Nicholson about Mosley or about the prospects for his political future. He wrote to Nicholson in June 1931:

I am very sorry to hear that you are getting more deeply involved in the New Party. I think the movement has petered out. It might be saved by immense sums of money, and brilliant journalistic support, but of course there is a conspiracy of silence in the newspapers, except for the particular newspapers I am connected with. I hope you will give up the New Party. If you must burn your fingers in public life, go to a bright and big blaze.

Beaverbrook was right. No amount of lunches at the Carlton Grill, or gatherings at Mosley's London house, or lobbying at All Souls could make up for the fact that when put to the test the new Party failed dismally. The British electorate did not take kindly to the corporate, organic state outlined by its adherents. Of the twenty four candidates all, including Mosley, were defeated. Twenty two forfeited their deposits and Harold Nicholson came fifth of five candidates with just 461 votes.

Left in a state of total confusion, Mosley and his party members were obliged to take stock. If the National Coalition government formed to combat the worsening economic situation succeeded in its task of effecting a recovery, the movement would cease to be new and would have to insinuate such valid ideas as it had into the political system by conventional means. If the government failed and the gulf between rich and poor widened to unacceptable proportions, a force would be needed to fight the alternative evil of communism. This force, Mosley became more and more convinced, must be fascism, for it was only by a combination of physical and political means that such an enemy could be conquered.

Many of Mosley's followers were not prepared to jump over this final idealogical hurdle; Harold Nicholson was one, John Strachey and Peter Howard were among others. Wrote Nicholson:

I am loyal to Tom since I have an affection for him. But I realise his ideas are different from my own. He had no political judgement. He believes in fascism. I don't. I loathe it. And I apprehend that the conflict between the intellectual and physical side of the N.P. may develop into something rather acute.

Mosley, on the other hand, felt no such scruples. If the only way to halt the decline of the Empire and to rescue Britain from the clutches of a flabby and weak-minded government was to inject a little discipline into his ranks, or to point out the folly of allowing the nation's Britishness to be polluted by outsiders, or to alert the people to the pernicious cancer of communism, then he would not falter in his self-appointed task.

One supporter ready to travel the thorny road of political outlawry, whose missionary fervour never flagged and whose personal adoration remained undimmed, was Diana Guinness, who eventually became his second wife. His first wife, Lady Cynthia Curzon, had had mixed feelings about her husband's bewildering changes of mood. They were married in the Chapel Royal in May 1920 and the wedding was the highlight of an otherwise drab season. King George V and Queen Mary, the King and Queen of Belgium, Mr Bonar Law and Lady Astor were among the guests who attended a lavish reception given by Lord Curzon at Carlton House Terrace after the ceremony. The happy pair were showered with expensive presents and Sir Oswald gave his bride a diamond tiara, a silver wristwatch, a diamond brooch and a sapphire ring. Lady Cynthia reciprocated with a set of pearl studs and pin and a golden wristwatch. After the honeymoon, which was spent in a castle above Portofino, they returned to their

Above: Mosley had an unfavourable reception when he spoke in Glasgow in 1931 as leader of the New Party.

betrayal was less a matter of idealism than a calculated move to further his own ends. "And then, after that, mind you, he suddenly went over to Labour",' wrote Amabel Williams-Ellis in *The Wall of Glass*. '"To Labour!" repeated the girl, mildly surprised. "Why?" "Vanity", answered Lady St Aubyn, succinctly. "He thought there would be less competition".'

Apart from the difficulties of expunging the stigma of desertion within his own class, Mosley had to put up with antagonism from his new allies, who were understandably suspicious of the gilded new cuckoo in their

Queen Anne house in Smith Square and Lady Cynthia settled down to being the wife of a rising public figure.

They were, of course, seen everywhere. Watched by eager gossip columnists they went to Ascot, to Deauville, to charity balls, to nightclubs and to country house parties. Lady Cynthia's looks and clothes were much remarked on by the *Tatler*, who described her as the 'personification of the society girl, tall, willowy, with a slightly bored expression, lovely complexion and expressive blue eyes' and waxed lyrical about her exquisite taste. Sir Oswald was described as 'handsome' and it was noted that 'as he jazzes round the room with his beautiful wife . . . his face is invariably wreathed in smiles.' The world was at their feet and the future was filled with the promise of endless delights and satisfactions. 'We rushed towards life with arms outstretched', wrote Mosley of that time, 'to embrace the sunshine, and even the darkness, the light and shade which is the essence of existence, every varied enchantment of a glittering wonderful world; a life rush to be consummated.'

Their contemporaries regarded them as a couple singled out by the gods for special favour and it came as a rude shock when first one and then the other took the treasonable step of defecting to the lower classes. The explanations, as far as Mosley was concerned, were not flattering. It was widely held that his nest. His wife, too, elegantly coiffured and smothered from head to foot in expensive furs, could hardly be said to represent the people. Lady Mosley, however, had always had a soft spot for the proletariat. She was, as Harold Nicholson said, 'profoundly working class at heart'; a quality put to practical use in 1929 when she stood as Labour candidate for Stoke and was elected. Loyalty to her husband impelled her to resign from the Labour Party in 1931 and she joined him in the New Party, although she was deeply antagonistic to his flirtation with the extreme right. 'Cimmie wants to put a notice in *The Times* to the effect that she dissociates herself from Tom's fascist tendencies', wrote Harold Nicholson in December 1931, adding, 'We pass it off as a joke.'

Far from being a joke, the effort of accommodating herself to such an alien ideology made her ill. A miscarriage followed by the premature birth of her third son in 1932 left her tired and debilitated. In 1933 she had an operation for an inflamed appendix, and two days later, on 16 May, she died of peritonitis.

Diana Guinness, whom Mosley had met while Lady Cynthia was still alive and while she was still married to the Hon Bryan Guin-

Below: Diana Mitford *(right)*, society beauty, married Oswald Mosley secretly in Berlin in 1936.

THE BLACK SHIRT DINNER

LADY RAVENSDALE AND COUNT
PAUL MUNSTER

COUNTESS MUNSTER AND
MAJOR METCALFE

LADY PETRIE AND SIR OSWALD
MOSLEY

CAPTAIN LUTTMAN-JOHNSON, CAPTAIN SIR THOMAS ROBINSON,
MR. R. D. BLUMENFELD AND MR. J. LEES-MILNE

SIR JOHN SQUIRE, SIR CHARLES PETRIE
AND MAUD, LADY MOSLEY

The January Club Dinner, which was a Black Shirt gathering, took place at the Savoy, and was notable for a very interesting debate between Sir Oswald Mosley, the originator of the Fascist movement in England, and Sir Charles Petrie, the famous historian and author of "The History of Government" and many other books, including "Mussolini." As might be expected, therefore, the debate was of a quite definitely serious nature. Sir Oswald Mosley is a brother-in-law of both Lady Ravensdale and Major "Fruity" Metcalfe, who married Lady Alexandra Curzon. Lady Cynthia Mosley was the third daughter of the late Lord Curzon of Kedleston, and, like her husband, a former Labour Member ; and Miss Aitken and Mr. W. Joyce, as will be noticed, were amongst those who strictly preserved the correct Black Shirt atmosphere. Literature and journalism were prominently represented by Sir John Squire, who is in the group with Sir Oswald Mosley's mother, and Mr. R. D. Blumenfeld

Photos: Swaebe

MR. W. JOYCE, DR. R. FORGAN AND MISS M. AITKEN

ness (later Lord Moyne), was born Diana Mitford. She was the fourth child of the seven talented children of Lord and Lady Redesdale, immortalized as 'Muv' and 'Farve' in her elder sister Nancy's novels, *The Pursuit of Love* and *Love in a Cold Climate*. After her marriage she became a society beauty, her perfect features staring regularly from the covers of glossy magazines, her comings and goings faithfully recorded in the *Tatler* and the *Lady*, her portrait painted by many fashionable artists, including Henry Lamb, Augustus John and John Banting. Young, high-spirited and extremely rich, she attracted the attention of a number of 'brilliantly amusing' people, among them Harold and William Acton, Brian Howard, Robert Byron, Evelyn Waugh, John Betjeman, John

Sutro, Roy Harrod, Randolph Churchill, Lytton Strachey, Emerald Cunard and Osbert Sitwell.

Like Imogen Quest, Adam Fenwick-Symes's imaginary socialite created to liven up his gossip column, she was the:

most lovely and popular of the young married set . . . witty and tender-hearted; passionate and serene, sensual and temperate, impulsive and discreet . . . and her set, the most intimate and brilliant in Europe [became a] byword for social inaccessability – the final goal for all climbers.

Evelyn Waugh dedicated *Vile Bodies* to her; C B Cochrane offered her the part of Perdita in *The Winter's Tale*; the celebrated hoax exhibition of paintings by a mysterious crippled German artist called Bruno Hat was staged at

Above: Evelyn Waugh dedicated *Vile Bodies* to Diana Mitford.

Far left: The Black Shirt Dinner as featured in the *Tatler* in 1934. Mosley's aristocratic background combined with his hypnotic voice converted many of the upper classes to his brand of positive politics.

Left: Putzi Hanfstaengl, the close supporter of Hitler who encouraged Diana Mitford to visit Germany and fostered her interest in the Nazi Movement.

her house in Buckingham Street (it was, of course, Brian Howard in disguise); and at the ball she gave for her twenty second birthday in 1931 'everyone they knew came, young and old, poor and rich, clever and silly.' Diana wore a pale grey dress of chiffon and tulle and 'all the diamonds' she could lay her hands on, and they all danced in the floodlit garden until dawn broke.

Unlike Imogen Quest, whose only aim was to be the most beautiful, the best dressed and the most adored woman of her generation, and to whom the social round was an end in itself, Diana Guinness harboured a longing for something more substantial. In Oswald Mosley she found everything she had been looking for. When she met him at a dinner party early in 1932, he cast a spell over her from which she never awoke. His absorption with great issues, and his certainty that he and he alone had the means to slay the hydra of unemployment and economic depression provided a heady antidote to all the frivolous chatter of the past years. 'He had every gift', she wrote in her memoirs, 'being handsome,

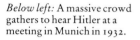

generous, intelligent and full of wonderful
gaiety and *joie de vivre*. Of course I fell in
love with him and decided to throw in my lot
with him.'

The decision made, she left her husband,
took a house in Eaton Square and prepared to
lead a life of secret devotion. Outwardly Lady
Cynthia Mosley's death changed little. Their
attachment was known only to a few close
friends and her interest in his movement was
considered to be just another eccentricity. In
the spring of 1933, however, the eccentricity
became an all-embracing obsession. Mrs
Richard Guinness invited Diana to 'come and
meet a very interesting German . . . a per-

sonal friend of Hitler.' His name was Putzi
Hanfstaengl and he, doutless captivated by
his fellow dinner guests's blond good looks
and serious attitude to National Socialism,
suggested that she should come to Germany
where he would introduce her to Hitler. 'You
will see with your own eyes', he said, 'what
lies are being told about us in your newspapers.'

Nothing loth, Diana, together with her
younger sister Unity, then aged nineteen, set
off a few months later for Bavaria. Herr Hanfstaengl had omitted to give them his address,
saying grandly that 'everybody in the new
Germany would know where to find him'

Above: Winifred Wagner, wife of Siegfried who directed annual productions of Wagner's music at Bayreuth. Winifred was introduced to the Mitford sisters in Bayreuth.

and it was only with some difficulty that they tracked him down in Nüremberg. He invited them to come to the *Parteitag* (party conference) which was then in progress, and which was the first one since Hitler had come to power. The following four days left them both drunk with excitement. The flags, the uniforms, the parades and the triumphant speeches completely turned their heads, and were some compensation for the fact that they never actually met Hitler. But they saw him and, as Diana Mosley wrote afterwards, when he appeared 'an almost electric shock passed through the multitude.'

The shock waves converged particularly strongly on Unity. As soon as she was back in England she badgered her parents without ceasing until they agreed to let her return to Germany to learn German so that when she finally met the Führer, as she was convinced she would, she would be able to understand what he said. A place was found for her with Baroness Laroche in Munich, a lady used to the ways of young English girls (Penelope and Angela Dudley Ward were among her favourites) and who was well acquainted with the infatuation many of them felt for Adolph Hitler.

Even the Baroness, however, was not pre-

Right: The theatre at Bayreuth. Hitler was devoted to Wagner's music, and attended the annual Wagner Festival held at Bayreuth.

pared for the single-mindedness of her latest charge. Not content with worshipping her hero from afar, she set out to attract his attention. At first she tried to enlist Dr Hanfstaengl's help but he refused on the grounds that his position as Hitler's foreign press chief was becoming compromised by the Mitford sisters' un-Nordic insistence on wearing rouge and lipstick at Party rallies. Undeterred, Unity found out that Hitler had a favourite restaurant in Munich, the Osteria Bavaria, and lay in wait for him there. Every Friday at lunchtime she sat at the nearest table she could to the hallowed spot where Hitler ate and gazed at him, according to a friend who was with her at the time, 'in blind adoration'. When, inevitably, he had to pass her by, she 'talked more loudly, or dropped a book' in the hope that he would notice her.

Eventually these tactics paid off, and Hitler, who in any case could hardly have failed to see Unity (she was six-foot tall) asked who she was. 'On learning that she was an English fräulein', wrote her younger sister Jessica, 'an admirer of the Nazis and a member of the British Union of Fascists [he] invited her to join them at their table.' Victorious at last, Unity wrote at once to Diana to tell her of her coup, and to urge her to come at once to Munich so that she could meet her illustrious new friend.

After that it was plain sailing. The two sisters became familiar figures at party rallies. In July 1936 they went to the Olympic Games in Berlin as the guests of Magda and Joseph Goebbels and later that summer to Bayreuth for the obligatory baptism by immersion in Wagner opera. During the long intervals they joined Hitler for supper at a restaurant near the Festspielhaus where, among others, they were introduced to the formidable Frau Winifred Wagner. Not for nothing had Unity been christened Unity Valkyrie.

These activities had not gone unnoticed by the press. The sight of Unity standing alongside the unprepossessing Gauleiter of Franconia, Julius Streicher (who had made a fortune from his anti-Semitic paper *Die Stürmer*), at a party rally at Hesselberg in June 1935, telling the vast throng that 'ordinary people in England have no idea of the Jewish danger' and assuring them that the English, too, would triumph over 'the world enemy', roused the *Daily Mirror* to print the headline 'Peer's daughter a Jew-Hater'. In September, having spotted that Unity was a guest of honour at the Congress of Nazi Groups Abroad, held at Erlangen in Bavaria, the British United Press noted that she and her sister had been given seats at the speaker's table where 'Julius Streicher, Germany's Jew-Baiter Number One was addressing the congress'. The *Frankische Tagezeitung*, on the other hand, remarked approvingly that the two English fascists 'had heard the Nazi message in their blood'.

Back in England, the *News Chronicle* found Diana, surrounded by a jeering, laughing, crowd, standing on a soap box in the middle of a demonstration in Hyde Park against German cruelties and persecutions. 'Mrs Guinness', they wrote, 'daughter of Lord Redesdale, stood in the crowd on her own and recorded a lone vote opposing resolutions refusing business relation with Germany and declining to buy German goods . . .' During the singing of 'God Save The King', she raised her arm in the fascist salute.

Considering the excellent copy Unity and Diana provided, it was surprising that Mosley and Diana were able to keep their friendship a secret for so long. It was not revealed until

Below: A German poster advertising the Winter Olympic Games. Hitler used the games as a propaganda exercise to demonstrate the superiority of the Aryan race and as an excuse to hold massive processions.

1938, when their first son, Alexander, was born. Meanwhile, in 1935, Mosley had installed Diana at Wootton, a remote country house in Staffordshire. On 6 October 1936, they were married in Berlin; the only place, Mosley claimed, with some justice, 'where [one] could get married without the Press hearing about it: an advantage of totalitarianism.' The ceremony took place in the drawing room of the Goebbels' house, and was attended by Hitler, who gave them a signed photograph of himself in a silver frame as a memento. It was the second and last time that Mosley met Hitler, the first being in Munich in 1935. Neither encounter was a great success. Mosley spoke no German, and Hitler was not an admirer of the leader of British fascism, maintaining that he was a poor substitute for the real thing.

The summer before the Mosleys' marriage, Lady Redesdale took Diana, Unity, Jessica and Deborah on a Mediterranean cruise. Lord and Lady Redesdale had watched their daughters' march to fascism with mixed feel-

ings – their natural curiosity was tempered by a strong feeling that the whole business was rather too theatrical for their taste. However once Unity and Diana had established themselves in Hitler's inner circle they implored their parents to come and visit them, so that they might taste the fruits of the gods and, fascinated despite themselves, the Redesdales gave in. Trips to the Osteria Bavaria and to Berlin followed and were a qualified success. There was the problem of the language, which neither had mastered, but set against that was the luxury of having their every whim indulged. 'Muv and Farve had a royal time in Germany', wrote Jessica in *Hons and Rebels*, 'They were lent a chauffeur-driven Mercedes-Benz and shown all the gaudy trappings of the new régime . . . they returned full of praise for what they had seen.'

Torn between Jessica, an emotional communist, and Unity and Diana, the Redesdales had a confusing time. Tempers became frayed during the cruise when Unity insisted on flaunting the gold swastika badge Hitler had given her, 'an outward and visible proof of inward devotion never relinquished' and which, in Spain in particular, gave rise to considerable hostility. As Jessica wrote:

She was surrounded by a hostile crowd shouting at her, clawing at her clothes, trying to tear off the hated symbol. Other cruise members hustled us back into the car, and we started the long, miserable journey back to the ship. On the way back Boud [Unity] and I had a furious quarrel which ended in a fist fight and hair-pulling match, and my mother crossly sent us to the cabin as soon as we boarded the cruise-ship.

Whether it was the memory of the glitter of her Berlin trip, or anger at these shipboard confrontations, Lady Redesdale openly sided with Diana against Jessica in these disputes. She ticked off the 'red' Duchess of Atholl, a fellow traveller on the cruise, who had given a lecture on 'Modern Despots' to the long-suffering passengers (who also had to put up with Unity rhapsodizing on the colour of Hitler's dressing gown), announcing that she

thought 'Nazism ... from every point of view preferable to communism'. The following year Jessica eloped with her cousin Esmond Romilly and went to Spain to work for the Nationalists. Lady Redesdale was more horrified by her political affiliations than by the danger to her life and limb, and the destroyer sent to fetch her was to rescue her from misguided principle rather than to save her skin.

Lord and Lady Redesdale were not by any means the only ones to be lulled into a false sense of security by the glamour of the new Germany. Chips Channon, another guest at the Olympic Games feted by Goebbels, Goering and the German Ambassador, von Ribbentrop, felt that 'we should let gallant little Germany glut her fill of the reds in the East and keep decadent France quiet while she does so. Otherwise we shall have not only reds in the West but bombs on London, Kelvendon and Southend.'

Nancy Astor, too, had many things to say about the state of affairs in Europe, which tripped off her garrulous tongue with a dreadful disregard for accuracy. She was reported by the *New York Times* as having said that 'the backers of anti-German feeling were overplaying their hands ... if the Jews are behind it they are going too far, and they need

to take heed.' She went on to declare that she was pro-Jew and have always been a Zionist but that she was 'against Communism ... Communism is the most horrible thing in the world. ...' and ending up by pointing out that the agitators against Germany ('and mind you I'm not all pro-German') were forgetting altogether the atrocities committed in other countries, in Russia, in Ethiopia and in Spain.

Dark intimations of fifth-columnist activity surrounded Lady Astor. Her weekend parties at Cliveden gave rise to rumours that she and Waldorf were the caucus of a powerful clique bent on active co-operation with Germany. Herr Ribbentrop had been seen coming and going. Lord Halifax came bustling down to Buckinghamshire to report on what he had found in Berlin; in November 1937 Nancy Astor wrote to Lord Lothian (later Ambassador-designate to Washington) that 'Edward Halifax came to luncheon the day after he returned from Germany. He liked everyone he met in Berlin and particularly Goebbels. ...'

Left-wing journalists, Claud Cockburn in particular, pounced on these sinister goings on, puffed them up, and tossed the inflated balloon of suspicion into the air. He forgot to mention that Lady Astor, shrewd as she was, was floundering in the shallows when it came to manipulating the ship of state through the muddy waters of appeasement. For Britain, rudderless and with a captain unable and unwilling to see the dangers ahead, was lurching rudderless towards the rocks. Nothing she could do could stop it. All anyone could do was to wait and see.

Previous page: British fascists salute Sir Oswald Mosley at a May Day Demonstration.

Far left: Lady Diana Cooper, drawn by D Low. Like many people, she was unable to face up to the changing world of the 1930s. The Wall Street Crash of 1929 brought problems for the rich, but desperate poverty for the poor.

Right: Germans raise their arms in the fascist salute in Berlin, 1934.

Below: Chamberlain flew to meet Hitler during the Munich Crisis of 1938. He acceded to all of Hitler's demands for the annexation of the Sudetenland, not realizing that Hitler would not be content with this expansion of German territory.

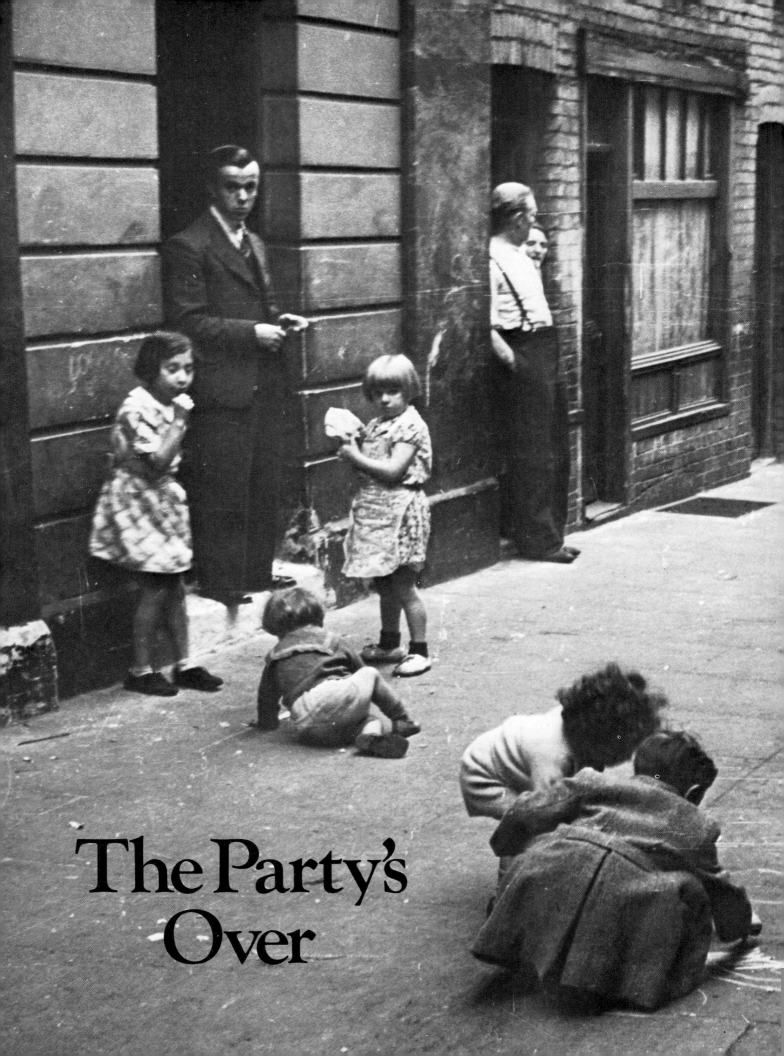

The Party's Over

'Was it in 1931, *annus terribilis*, that the pound fell?' asked Lady Diana Cooper in her memoirs. 'Whenever it was, Duff and I were in Dorset staying with the Cranbornes. Lord and Lady Salisbury were of the party, and so were Mr Baldwin and others. . . .' There was some talk, after the news that the pound had fallen, of short rations and sacrifice and stiff upper lips, but such pessimism was not to be tolerated for long. 'Were the dejected or the buoyant right', she continued, 'I have never asked, nor have I thought of it again.'

Lady Diana was not alone in her reluctance to face up to the unpleasant fact that the economy was showing signs of cracking under the strain induced by the Wall Street Crash on 24 October 1929. The sight of the most prosperous nation on earth being brought to

its knees by greedy financiers and ignorant amateur speculators shocked the whole of the Western world. When first England and then America went off the gold standard and the ripples of financial insecurity washed over the Atlantic, bringing panic and corruption, shock turned to alarm.

The repercussions of these fluctuations in the American money market and the havoc they wreaked on world trade affected everyone with a stake in the economy. Inevitably, however, it affected the poor rather than the rich. The rich, in America as well as in England, remained cocooned in their private world, their problems ones of compromise rather than of necessity. While small-time investors were hurling themselves from tower blocks or taking overdoses of aspirin in order to escape from the humiliation and despair of bankruptcy and 14,000,000 unemployed were thrown onto the mercy of an uncaring nation, American financiers were wondering whether they should reinforce their town houses with bullet-proof shutters or whether Amsterdam or Geneva was a better repository for the money they had left. Between 1931 and 1933, according to Neil Vanderbilt, not less than two billion gold dollars were transferred to Switzerland, thus bringing about the 'worst panic ever experienced in America'. Raising cash became a fetish among American multi-millionaires, and allegiance to the preservation of their living standards the only creed worth fighting for. It was a distasteful sight, even for one of their own class. Mr Vanderbilt wrote:

They stopped at nothing. They sold "at the market" huge blocks of stocks and bonds. They forced the heads of mortgage companies to lend them millions of dollars on their real-estate holdings. They withdrew every cent they had on deposit with out-of-town banks. They borrowed on jewellery, yachts, and motor cars. The series of breaks which occurred in the stock market in the fall of 1931 owed its origin to that cry of "On to Amsterdam and Basle" with which Society returned from Newport and Southampton in the closing days of the month of September 1931. Nothing mattered to them but "liquidity". Nothing could have checked their maniacal activities except a prompt embargo on any and all gold shipments.

This embargo, as Mr Vanderbilt pointed out, would have been unlikely to materialize, since it could only have been implemented by those whose interests least encouraged them to do so.

Perhaps the most telling sign of the times in New York was the decision to leave the Metropolitan Opera Company to its own devices. Bogged down by lack of cash (it all having been converted into Swiss francs or Dutch gulden), large numbers of well-heeled sub-

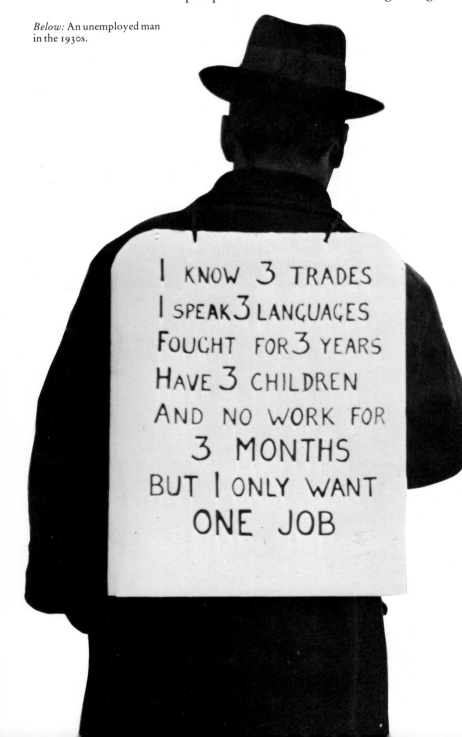

Below: An unemployed man in the 1930s.

Above: A family in Bethnal Green, one of London's poor areas, in 1923.

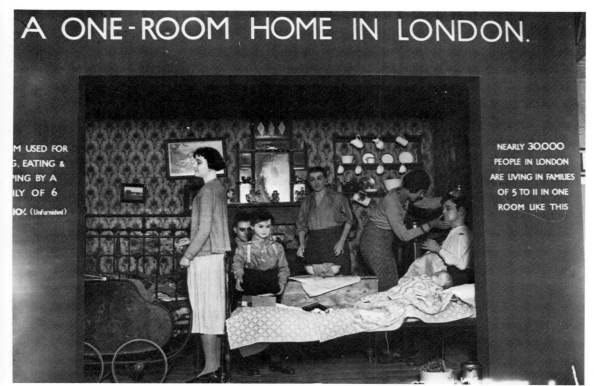

A ONE-ROOM HOME IN LONDON.

...M USED FOR ...G, EATING & ...PING BY A ...ILY OF 6 ...10% (Unfurnished)

NEARLY 30,000 PEOPLE IN LONDON ARE LIVING IN FAMILIES OF 5 TO 11 IN ONE ROOM LIKE THIS

Left: A wax model of a typical overcrowded slum which appeared at the Housing and Building Trades Exhibition in London in 1932.

scribers withdrew their support and the company was floated on the open market. Justifications for this at upper-crust dinner tables ranged from annoyance that they no longer dared to wear their jewellery in public to fear of a Soviet takeover. 'Let them remove the bread-line from the vicinity of the Metropolitan first. Fancy my driving past that mob wearing my emeralds' and 'Subscribe for the 1933-34 season? Not on your life. For all I know the Soviets will be here by then . . .' were some of the more restrained comments.

To launch the appeal for the opera house's salvation society ladies went on the radio to put out an SOS for the company, inviting anyone with anything at all to 'kick-in their nickels and dimes'. Neil Vanderbilt observed:

Few events in modern history were as disgusting and as revealing in their boundless hypocrisy as that Save the Metropolitan Drive conducted by the millionaires among the paupers. . .The money spent on food and champagne served at lunches and dinners given for the sole purpose of discussing "that Metropolitan thing" would have been sufficient to finance an entire unabbreviated Season of the Opera, but money was not the issue, only a smoke screen. The box holders who "graciously consented" to make a radio appeal could have raised the necessary sum in five minutes through the simple medium of producing their own cheque-books, but that would have deprived them of a glorious opportunity to prove to "the Soviets" that there was no money left on Fifth Avenue . . .

The cries of anguish from American dowagers were equalled by the grumbles that reverberated among the inhabitants of Eaton and Belgrave Square in August 1931, when it became apparent that the British economy had been infected by the unstable state of affairs in New York. The report of the May Committee on national expenditure forecast a budget deficit of $120 million, foreign investors became alarmed and withdrew funds, Government securities depreciated and panic borrowing resulted. To combat these dangerous developments a National Government was formed, drawing support from all three par-

Far left: An unemployed man in the 1930s. Precipitated by the Wall Street Crash of 1929, unemployment rose to 2,745,000 in 1932 in Britain, and did not fall significantly until the start of World War II.

Below: A court dress of the 1930s. Despite financial difficulties, the rich did not suffer during the Great Depression, and the Season continued unabated.

ties. On 6 October a General Election was held in order to quell dissent from a number of Labour and Liberal members who refused to co-operate with this scheme on the grounds that they had been press-ganged into it against their will. The country, however, responded to the appeal for a 'doctor's mandate' and the National Government was returned to power with 554 seats.

With a mandate to govern and with Ramsay MacDonald as its Prime Minister, the National Government set about putting things to rights – watched with a considerable amount of gloom by the upper classes who now had to face unpalatable sacrifices such as higher taxation and the introduction of death duties. The *Queen* went a stage further, predicting, if not quite the end of the world, then the end of civilization, at least as embodied by London Society:

The pessimist tells us to prepare for the worst . . . that the world depression has by no means reached its climax, and that we have many anxious months possibly years ahead. They say that civilisation is a failure and that there is practically no hope left of any satisfactory solution to our problems.

Fortunately for the world, and for London Society in particular, these Cassandrian prophecies did not come to pass. Civilization, which for the readers of the *Queen* centred around the London Season and a plentiful supply of servants, only fell apart very slightly at the seams. Some London clubs were obliged to close, Ranelagh was bought by Ansbachers for building develoment – a speculation that later failed, much to the delight of elderly roués who remembered stolen hours driving the lady of their choice down to the river to take tea before the war – Daly's theatre shut down and many London houses were turned into business premises. The servant problem, a phenomenon brought about by the change in women's employment during the First World War, was not, as might have been expected, solved by the rise in unemployment. Parlourmaids and kitchen maids were still difficult to find and obstinate in their demands for more money and better living conditions. The *Queen* wrote disapprovingly in 1931 that 'the social status of the servant is very largely to blame for the fact that though there is so much unemployment, young women refuse to enter our houses', adding inconsistently that it would be a charitable act if every household took on extra help during the dark days of depression. Even more inconsistently it advised hard-pressed ladies of the house to look abroad for domestic help, although they thought that Mrs Sacheverell Sitwell was 'a little extreme' in having a black nanny for her children.

The Season continued unabated, depres-sion or no depression. Some sacrifices were made: King George V set an example by taking a cut in the civil list; a few well-disposed ladies set about brightening up what was euphemistically called 'the enforced leisure' of the unemployed by manning soup kitchens or running social clubs in deprived areas; the Prince of Wales toured the mining disricts of South Wales; and some militant undergraduates turned to Marxism. However the majority of the upper class dug their heads firmly in the sand, preferring to echo the sentiments of the columnist who wrote in 1931 that:

The London Season is undoubtedly one of the seven wonders of the modern world. People said it would never survive the war, that modern youth did not want set entertainments in the grand manner, dignity, tradition, but they were wrong, for here in 1931 the season is starting again to run its triumphant course through the summer . . . Eton and Harrow Match, the Royal Garden Party, and now Cowes and Scotland and cures and things that people do who make the round of the seasons. . . .

The splendour of the Duchess of Sutherland's arrangements in London, at Hampden House and at Dunrobin were much admired. 'Aloof

Right: One of Britain's 1,830,000 unemployed tries to find a job in 1939. He drew just over two pounds a week in benefit.

Below: Massive unemployment in Germany was partly responsible for Hitler's rise to power.

and beautiful', the *Queen* wrote in 1936, 'her plans for entertaining are seldom made public. She has wonderful jewels and knows how to wear them. She travels by car or in a private plane.' In 1937 the Duchess gave a very public ball for the newly crowned King George VI and Queen Elizabeth, the first time since the war that a reigning monarch had attended a private dance – a democratic move that earned them loud cheers from the crowd who waited outside Hampden House to see the royal couple arrive and depart. As far as the writers of gossip columns could see, everything was the same as ever.

Such ostrich-like behaviour was not confined to the state of affairs at home. Unpleasant rumours of upheavals abroad had begun to infiltrate across the Channel, dismissed by most as the manoeuvres of a handful of megolomaniacs, posing little threat to that panacea for all international ills, the League of Nations. In 1935 the Japanese invaded Manchuria, in 1936 the Italians laid claim to Abyssinia and the same year German troops, under their new Chancellor Adolf Hitler, marched into the demilitarized Rhineland. These flagrant acts of aggression caused less of a stir than might be supposed. Even after it became patently obvious that the League was unable to prevent Japan from doing what it liked, hopes were held up for its mollifying effect on Benito Mussolini and Adolf Hitler. The *Queen* wrote blandly that 'although Italian troops have been shipped to Africa, it is improbable that the nation would really wish an armed conflict with Abyssinia, possibly Mussolini himself least of all.' It was equally keen to look on the bright side when Hitler removed Germany from the League altogether, counselling moderation and expressing the opinion that 'if this course is followed, Germany, seeing the solidarity of world opinion, may yet return to the League and ask for the revision of the treaties in a peaceful and acceptable fashion.'

The *Queen* remained doggedly biased in favour of the two dictators long after they had

lost all credence in the eyes of most of the rest of the British press. Mussolini was a great favourite and could do little wrong. Just before the Abyssinian invasion he was hailed as a peacemaker and just afterwards he was excused on the grounds that although he undoubtedly had a desire for power 'there was nothing self-seeking about him.' In 1933 he was nominated as 'one of the current personalities likely to become an immortal, along with the Prince of Wales, Charlie Chaplin and the Chief Scout', and he had been much praised for turning Capri into a bird sanctuary, which touched British hearts.

Hitler was a less sympathetic figure, but even he had redeeming features. Not very much was said about his attitude to the Jews. It was considered that most of the stories of atrocities were either exaggerated or untrue, and that in any case the Jewish problem was one that Germans had to solve for themselves. The *Queen* dwelt heavily on the Chancellor's vigorous qualities, his ability to get Germany working again and his kindness to animals – his prohibition of vivisection prompted many approving letters.

Not only the *Queen* sought to soften the

unacceptable face of German aggression. Neville Chamberlain, Prime Minister since 1937, was bent on bringing Germany to heel by peaceful negotiation. In this he was supported by all those who thought the terms of the Treaty of Versailles had been too harsh, that Germany had a right to equality in armaments and to a place in Europe, and who felt that the Germans of Austria, Czechoslovakia and Poland had a right to self-determination. He was also supported by those who had decided, with the members of the Oxford Union Debating Society, that there were no circumstances under which they could be persuaded to fight for King and country, and whose dislike of violence and distaste for war profiteers had turned them into pacifists and appeasers. Almost everyone, left and right, old and young, convinced themselves that the dark cloud of fascism would roll away. The Left put its faith in the Soviet Union, believing that moral disapproval would shame fascist Germany and oblige it to abandon its undemocratic ways, the Right upheld the status quo and believed in the stabilizing influence of the empire, the old supported the Right and the young veered this way and that. A few solitary voices were raised against the folly of not upsetting the peaceful apple cart at any price, but they were howled down as the doom-laden prophecies of self-interested warmongers.

After a while it became apparent to even the most dedicated upholders of the status quo that neither Mussolini nor Hitler were open to reason. Mussolini, counted on to help save Austria from German domination in return for British rcognition of his empire in Abyssinia, did nothing at all when Hitler marched into Vienna on 13 March 1938. Negotiations over Czechoslovakia similarly came to grief. Chamberlain persuaded himself that he had come to an agreement with Hitler over self-determination for the Germans in the Sudeten Land, but he failed to grasp, or did not want to see, that Hitler had designs on the whole of Czechoslovakia. On 29 September 1938 he flew to Munich to settle the business and returned triumphant, having papers that guaranteed the future of the Sudeten Land and ensured that Britain and Germany would conduct their affairs in the future through consultation, not war. The lion had lain down with the lamb, and swords had been beaten into ploughshares; it was a victory for the counsellors of moderation and good sense.

One by one, however, illusions to Right and Left were shattered. The champions of appeasement saw their faith in honourable agreements eroded with merciless disregard when Hitler moved into Prague in March 1939, and members of the extreme Left who had worshipped at the shrine of communism

Left: Newspaper sellers in Piccadilly Circus announce the invasion of Poland and Britain's consequent mobilization.

The QUEEN

THE LADY'S NEWSPAPER & COURT CHRONICLE

Established 1861

me 185. No. 4838

Wednesday, September 13th, 193

Photo: MARCUS ADAMS

THEY ARE MOTHER AND FATHER, TOO

*King George and Queen Elizabeth, while they are playing a big part in the life of this strange
new London, must often find their thoughts turning, just as those of other parents are doing,
to the two little daughters they have had to leave behind in the greater safety of the country*

saw the Soviet Union ally itself in a pact with Germany against Great Britain and France. On the night of 2 September 1939 German troops crossed the Polish border and German aeroplanes bombed Warsaw. There was no more shelter to be had under the umbrella of appeasement. An attempt was made to deliver an ultimatum to the German government, suggesting a conference if they would withdraw their troops from Poland without delay, but the ultimatum expired at eleven o'clock in the morning of 3 September. The Germans did not reply and at five o'clock in the afternoon Britain declared war.

On 2 September Duff Cooper, who a year before had resigned as First Lord of the Admiralty in protest at the terms of the Munich Agreement, was having a drink in the clubhouse of the Goodwood golf course, when he heard one man saying to another 'Hitler started on Poland this morning'. 'That was how I heard', he wrote in his diary, 'that the Second World War had begun.' In the afternoon he and Lady Diana drove to London and had dinner with Winston Churchill at the Savoy Grill. After dinner they went out into the street plunged into total darkness by the blackout and were nearly run over by a large car. Inside was Bendor, Duke of Westminster. On their way home, Bendor told them how much he admired Hitler, how much he disliked the Jewish race and how pleased he was that the country was not yet at war, adding that 'Hitler knew, after all, that we were his friends'. It was too much for Duff Cooper. According to Lady Diana he turned on his benefactor and said, 'I hope that by tomorrow he will know that we are his most implacable and remorseless enemies.' Bendor remained unrepentant. Next day, Lady Diana wrote, he telephoned a friend to tell them that 'if there were a war it would be entirely due to the Jews and Duff Cooper.'

Right up to the actual declaration of war the *Queen* tried to believe that it could never happen. When it did, the magazine stuck firmly to the bare essentials, expressing regret that the King and Queen would have their holiday arrangements upset for the second year in succession and hoping that that 'rascal Hitler' would be seen off for good and all so that things could get back to normal.

It was a small gesture of defiance against the forces of darkness that were rising up over the horizon. Nobody knew what the future held, but of one thing the upper classes were sure. Nothing would ever be the same again. How could it be? For the past twenty years the whole upper tenth of a nation had lived with the 'insouciance of grand dukes and the casualness of chorus girls'. It had been 'the age of miracles . . . of art . . . of excess!' But, as Scott Fitzgerald said, it had been borrowed time.

Far left: The Royal Family as featured in the *Queen* on 13 September 1939, just a few days after the outbreak of World War II. Along with many other Londoners, they sent their children to the country because of the fear of air raids.

Left: A newsboy announces the start of World War II.

Index

Acknowledgements

The author and publisher would like to thank the following people who have helped in the preparation of this book: Jane Laslett, the editor; David Eldred, the designer; Wendy Sacks, who carried out the picture research; Penny Murphy, who prepared the index.

Picture Credits

The pictures were supplied by the **BBC Hulton Picture Library** except for the following:
Bison Picture Library: 129 (bottom), 100 (bottom), 186/7.
Bundesarchiv: 182 (both), 191, 198.
Country Life: 31 (left), 146 (top).
Geffrye Museum: 120.

The Illustrated London News Picture Library: 8 (top), 21 (top), 22 (top), 23 (top), 24 (top), 29 (bottom left), 30 (bottom), 40 (top), 43 (top), 46 (bottom), 52, 56/7, 69 (top right), 78, 79, 109 (top), 114 (top right and bottom left), 116 (both), 117 (both), 121 (top left and bottom), 122 (all), 123, 124 (top), 125, 126/7, 128, 131 (both), 133, 134/5, 138 (both), 152 (both), 153, 155 (top), 156 (bottom), 157, 162 (both), 163, 165, 177, 178 (top), 180.
Imperial War Museum: 20 (bottom).
Leeds City Art Galleries: back jacket.
London Transport: front jacket, 121

(top right), 124 (bottom left and bottom right).
The Raymond Mander and Joe Mitchenson Theatre Collection: 86, 90 (both), 92 (top), 94, 96, 98 (top left and top right), 99 (top left and top right), 114 (top left and bottom right).
Mansell Collection: 130 (top left).
Millar and Harris: 63 (bottom), 64 (bottom), 65 (bottom), 67 (both), 68 (top and bottom right).
Museum of London: 9 (bottom right), 113, 118/9.
National Magazine Company: 204.
National Portrait Gallery: 29 (bottom right), 62, 74 (left), 76 (both), 77 (bottom), 80 (left), 173 (bottom), 181 (top), 182, 186 (both), 190 (top).

National Railway Museum, York: 126 (top).
Jerry Ohlinger's Movie Material: 100 (top), 102 (bottom).
The Photo Source/Fox: 2/3.
The Photo Source/Keystone: 50/51.
Sotheby's London (Cecil Beaton): 36 (top), 59 (top), 60 (both), 64 (top), 65 (top), 68 (bottom left), 70/71, 77 (top), 81, 82 (bottom), 83, 84, 101, 142/3, 147, 164, 166/7.
Paul Tanqueray: 146 (bottom).
The Tate Gallery, London: 115, 127 (top).
Victoria and Albert Museum: 20 (top).
Julian Vinogradoff: 72 (both), 73 (bottom), 74 (right), 85.